Customer Service
Career Success
through
Customer Satisfaction

----------------   ------------------

PAUL R. TIMM

The Marriott School of Management
Brigham Young University

Prentice Hall, Upper Saddle River, NJ 07458

Library of Congress Cataloging-in-Publication Data

Timm, Paul R.
  Customer service : career success through customer satisfaction /
Paul R. Timm.
    p.   cm.
  Includes bibliographical references and index.
  ISBN 0-13-576695-8 (pbk.)
  1. Customer services.   2. Consumer satisfaction.   3. Customer
relations.   4. Success in business.   I. Title.
HF5415.5.T513   1997
658.8' 12—dc21   97–14962
                                                                  CIP

Acquisition Editor: Elizabeth Sugg
Editorial/production supervision, interior design,
    and electronic page makeup: Mary Araneo
Editorial Assistant: Emily Jones
Marketing Manager: Danny Hoyt
Director of Production and Manufacturing: Bruce Johnson
Managing Editor: Mary Carnis
Manufacturing Manager: Ed O'Dougherty
Cover Designer: Joe Sengotta

© 1998 Prentice-Hall, Inc.
Simon & Schuster/A Viacom Company
Upper Saddle River, New Jersey 07458

Printed in the United States of America

10 9 8 7 6 5 4 3 2 1

ISBN 0-13-576695-8

Prentice-Hall International (UK) Limited, *London*
Prentice-Hall of Australia Pty. Limited, *Sydney*
Prentice-Hall Canada Inc., *Toronto*
Prentice-Hall Hispanoamericana, S.A., *Mexico*
Prentice-Hall of India Private Limited, *New Delhi*
Prentice-Hall of Japan, Inc., *Tokyo*
Simon & Schuster Asia Pte. Ltd., *Singapore*
Editora Prentice-Hall do Brasil, Ltda., *Rio de Janeiro*

Contents

iii

Preface

This book is written in response to a need for a different approach to learning the skills needed to succeed in the challenging arena of customer service.

The other customer service books displayed in bookstores everywhere typically take one of two forms: They either tell the story of one company's efforts at boosting service quality, or they reveal a series of tips and ideas. These are fine as far as they go. I have written several such books myself. And books like this can have value so long as the reader effectively translates the ideas into application for his or her organization. But these books seldom show how to apply these diverse ideas to your organization.

The few textbooks available in customer service tend to offer oversimplified suggestions on how to phrase conversations, how to smile and be polite with customers, and the like. Their simplicity defies the real world where real people don't speak from scripts and real human relationships are complex and ever-changing.

This book takes a different approach. It ties together the best information from bookstore trade books and school textbooks—and then adds more. In this book you will find a clear and usable process for developing the kinds of skills, attitudes, and thinking patterns needed to win customer satisfaction and loyalty. The process includes developing

- a heightened awareness of the challenges and opportunities,
- the tools for dealing with unhappy customers by using the power of customer expectations and by creating loyalty
- the ability to lead, expand, and empower the service process
- specific skills for professional success, and
- a clear understanding of the future directions of customer service.

Perhaps no arena offers as much opportunity for organizational and professional success as customer service. It lies at the heart of any organization's reason to exist. The companies that do it well experience enormous profitability, marketplace acceptance, and genuine satisfaction among their employees.

Apply *Customer Service* and enjoy the rewards of professional excellence. Then, let me know how you applied the ideas. I can be reached at e-mail: DrTimm@AOL.com or fax: (810) 378-8309.

ACKNOWLEDGMENTS

The author and editor would like to thank the following commentators for their expert reviews: Garland Keesling, Towson State University; Shek True, Fort Lewis College.

The Role
of Customer Service
in Your Success

Do it, or die!

> Great service is about attitude. And a service attitude leads to a richer quality of life, not only in the commercial sector.
>
> — Leonard Berry[1]

THE WAY IT IS . . .

Writer Peter Glen relates an incident that too clearly reflects the kind of service people have to tolerate today:

> Early one morning in America, hungry, alone, and lost in the land of no customer service, I stumbled into a Dunkin' Donuts in Connecticut. The parking lot was dirty and the trash cans overflowed, but the parking lot was already full of cars and the trash cans would see more, much more. Inside were lines of people smoking cigarettes and wearing parkas, waiting to buy donuts. I waited with them, observing the uncleared counter where I soon would sit to eat my donut. It hadn't been cleared recently, and it wasn't going to be cleared now.
>
> I reached the head of the line, came face to face with a seventeen-year-old girl who had been condemned to serve me. Something in her seventeen-year-old face told me that all was not well in America's service economy. I asked her how she liked her job.
>
> She looked me straight in the eye and said, "It sucks!"

> That's service in America. And it's too bad, because we are a "service economy." But we don't give good service and we don't get it. We expect poor quality and bad service, and we are rarely disappointed.
>
> Instead of fighting, we whine. Those who provide service whine about the people they hire and the people they hire pass the whining right down to their customers. Those who buy service—customers—whine right back.[2]

Customer satisfaction horror stories—many far worse than just shabby donut-shop service—are everywhere. We've all come to expect less than optimal service despite the claims that we live in a service economy. It is tempting to join the chorus of complainers and no one will criticize you if you do. But we can also look at this state of affairs from another viewpoint: as an opportunity. The upside potential for those who give good service is unlimited. By making the process of customer satisfaction a part of our daily lives, we can virtually guarantee our professional and career success.

-------------------- *Learning Objectives* --------------------

When you have studied this chapter you should be able to

1. Recognize the validity of the statement, "No business or organization can succeed unless it creates customer loyalty."

2. Define "customer" and understand the complexity of various customer relationships.

3. Describe the nature of internal and external customers and identify some key constituencies you need to serve in order to achieve your personal and career goals.

4. Roughly calculate the cost of a lost customer.

5. Understand the advantages of keeping current customers versus an overemphasis on attracting new ones.

6. Recognize the dilemma faced by organizations whose lowest-paid employees are the customer's only interface with the company.

7. Explain what is and what is not customer loyalty.

8. Buy into the notion that customer service is indeed a master key to career success.

NO ONE SUCCEEDS WITHOUT CUSTOMER SATISFACTION

No business or organization can succeed without building customer satisfaction and loyalty. Likewise, no person can make a good living without meeting the needs of customers.

Those statements may seem to be rather broad generalizations, but let's consider this argument a bit further. Most people would agree that a business needs customers—however, not everyone works in business. What about other kinds of organizations? Does a government agency need customer satisfaction to succeed? Does a civic organization, church congregation, political party, family, service club, school, or fraternity need satisfied customers to succeed?

To answer these questions, we need first to define what we mean by a customer. The common perception is that a customer is someone who buys something from you.

> A "customer" can be broadly defined as a person with whom we exchange value.

Most people assume that to buy involves the exchange of money for something. True enough. But a broader view of "customer" may be more useful. In its broadest sense a customer is *someone with whom we exchange value.*

CUSTOMERS BY ANY OTHER NAME . . .

We have a lot of names for customers, often varying by the nature of our business or organization. Some examples: clients, patients, passengers, patrons, members, associates, insureds, users, buyers, subscribers, readers, viewers, purchasers, end-users, patrons, guests, cases, and yes, even students.

The commonality in all these customers is that they engage in some sort of transaction with us or our organization. They give us something (often, but not always, money) in exchange for something of value (usually services or goods).

The different names we use for customers convey various goods or services provided. For example, a typical *client* relationship usually implies something more complex and ongoing than, say, a customer of a convenience store. A higher level of *service intimacy* exists between a consultant and her client. The notion that a student is a customer is gaining grudging acceptance in academia. The relationship here is quite different than, say, a passenger who purchases transportation. The professor engages in a transaction to be sure. In exchange for tuition money he or she gives the student/customer information. But the relationship gets more complex when one considers that the professor also gives or withholds certification that a student has

> Different names for customers can imply different kinds of transactions.

mastered some material. This reflects a higher service intimacy. In other words, one cannot just buy a college education via a simple cash-for-a-degree exchange.

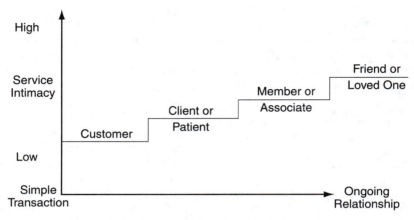

Figure 1–1 Levels of "Customer" Relationships

Similarly, a physician's patient is both a health-care buyer and one who chooses whether or not he or she wants to really "consume" the doctor's product. Dealing with the doctor can be a life-changing event with high service intimacy. Calling this critical relationship just another customer exchange may, in the eyes of some, cheapen it. The professional bears an obligation of stewardship that exceeds what is implied in the broader term "customer" used here.

Figure 1-1 shows examples of the kinds of terms we use to refer to the customer under different levels of service intimacy and relationship development. The further we move to the upper right section of the chart, the more crucial the customer-service process becomes.

CUSTOMERS AS PARTNERS

Relationships with customers can evolve into rich and fulfilling partnerships. Consultant-author Chip Bell contends that such a customer partnership arises from certain attitudes or orientations. Among these, he says that such partnerships are

- anchored in an attitude of generosity, a "giver" perspective that finds pleasure in extending the relationship beyond just meeting a need or requirement
- grounded in trust
- bolstered by a joint purpose
- marked by truth, candor, and straight talk mixed with compassion and care

- based on balance and pursuit of equality (I'll talk more about this in Chapter 4)
- grounded in grace, which Bell describes as "an artistic flow that gives participants a sense of familiarity and ease.[3]

Not every customer relationship becomes a partnership, of course. But such partnerships represent the highest level of customer-provider affiliation.

Notwithstanding the semantic distinctions about customers, it remains useful to agree that everyone has customers—we interact with people who depend upon us to provide them with information, guidance, services, products, or social support. In exchange for these, we give something back. This exchange system defines, on the most basic level, what it means to be a customer. When this exchange evolves into something more—when we move up the steps of service intimacy and relationship building—we'll enjoy immense levels of career and personal satisfaction.

> The "customer-as-partner" reflects a high level relationship.

CUSTOMERS IN SOCIAL EXCHANGES

Let's get back to basics for a moment. As human beings we are constantly exchanging value with each other. We are, by nature, social beings. We give and take from one another. When we exchange money for a product or service we are customers. When we provide work in exchange for a wage our boss and our company are our customers. When we participate in a civic organization or church group, the people to whom we give support, advice, ideas, information and the like are our customers. When we give of ourselves to contribute to a strong family, our spouse, parents, kids and others become our customers. When we build and maintain networks of friends and associates we become each others' customers.

> The broader view of the term customer reminds us that customer service skills can be widely applied to all aspects of life.

By accepting this broader view of what it means to be and have customers, we will see that applying the principles of customer service results in much more than business or financial success. Customer service is a key to career success but, more importantly, it is a master key to success in all phases of one's life. By applying the customer service principles in this book to every aspect of your life, you will gain exceptional levels of success and life-satisfaction.

Customer service skill is the master key to success.

Customer service skills—the ability to create value—are easy to develop and apply. Your success depends largely on your attitude and a willingness to try new behaviors. By mastering key skills you'll get the kinds of results that will help you achieve new levels of success.

GETTING AND KEEPING CUSTOMERS

Let's assume for a moment that you have started a new business. You see a demand for your products or services and you've lined up your first few customers. Without customers—people willing to exchange something of value for the products or services your business is offering—your venture won't last long. Some enterprises can exist with only a few customers, but most find it advantageous to get a larger customer base.

New customers can be tough to get. An oft-quoted statistic says that it costs five or six times as much to get a new customer than to keep an existing one. So logically, it makes sense to focus on satisfying customers you already have, thus encouraging repeat business. Barring that, you'll spend a lot of time and effort refilling a leaky bucket as you chase an ever-replenishing supply of new customers. (This is the dilemma faced by companies that offer shoddy products. People may buy from them one time but will not come back.)

Getting new customers and replacing those lost is an expensive part of any business.

Some people think that advertising is a good way to induce people to buy. In fact, U.S. business spends about $11.5 billion a year on advertising. Yet a recent survey showed that only 25 percent of those polled said that a television ad would induce them to buy. Likewise only 15 percent and 13 percent respectively

Customer service is like a daily election and customers vote with their feet.

said that newspaper or magazine ads caused them to buy. In short, traditional advertising has little confidence among consumers. Advice or the recommendation from a friend or relative, however, scored 63 percent as a determinant of people's buying a new product.[4] This confirms what people have long known: Word-of-mouth is still the best way to attract customers.

To sustain repeat business it is important to generate positive word-of-mouth "advertising" with great service. People talk to others about a service experience when it is exceptional, out of the ordinary. You can have the best products available, but if you fail to supplement them with a positive service experience, few people will notice the difference between you and your competition. Service success is a matter of setting yourself apart from other sources of products through unexpected excellence.

> Advertising is less effective at getting customers than positive word-of-mouth.

Good News and Bad News . . .

Across the economy, organizational results with customers offers both bad and good news—both pain and opportunity.

First the bad news. The average American company will lose 10 percent to 30 percent of its customers this year—mostly because of poor service. When customers have a choice, they'll go to the competition up to one third of the time. Customer satisfaction is like an election held everyday, and the people vote with their feet. If dissatisfied, they walk (sometimes run) to your competitor. When customers don't have a choice—such as in dealing with public utilities or government agencies—they'll use their feet for something else: they'll kick back!

Now the good news. Organizations that initiate effective customer retention programs have seen profits jump 25 to 100 percent. Non-profit groups see reduced turnover, better financial results, and happier staffs. Like it or not, customer service will always be the decisive battleground where winners and losers are quickly sorted out.

THE TERRIBLE COST OF THE LOST CUSTOMER

What happens when we give poor service and the customer quits being a customer? Most people don't understand the real cost of a lost customer. When an unhappy customer decides to stop doing business with us, the costs are much more than we realize.

To get a clearer view of the cost impact of a lost customer, let's consider a business we are all familiar with: a grocery supermarket. Here's a story of Mrs. Williams:[5]

Harriet Williams, a sixty-something single woman, has been shopping at Happy Jack's Super Market for many years. The store is close to home and its products competitively priced. Last week, Mrs. Williams approached the produce manager and said, "Sonny, can I get a half head of lettuce." He looked at her like she was crazy and curtly said, "Sorry, lady. We just sell the whole head." She was a bit embarrassed but accepted his refusal.

Later she had several other small disappointments (she wanted a quart of skim milk and they only had half-gallons) and when she checked out her groceries she was largely ignored by the clerk who was carrying on a conversation with a fellow employee. The clerk made matters worse by abruptly demanding "two forms of ID" with Harriet's check (What do they think I am, a common criminal?) and failing to say thank you.

Mrs. Williams stepped out of the store that day and decided that she was no longer going to do business there. Although she had shopped at Happy Jack's for many years, she realized that she had never felt that her business was appreciated. She got the overall feeling that Happy Jack's employees could care less if she shopped there. She spent about 50 hard-earned dollars there every week, but to the store employees she was just another cash cow to be milked without so much as a sincere "thank you." Nobody seemed to care whether she was a satisfied customer. But today is different—no more "nice" Mrs. Williams! Today she decided to buy her groceries elsewhere. Maybe—just maybe—there is a store where they'll appreciate her business.

Goodbye, Mrs. Williams.

Express gratitude often. Without customers you have no business, no job.

What do the employees think about that? They're not worried. Life is like that. You win some; you lose some. Happy Jack's is a pretty big chain and doesn't really need Mrs. Williams. Besides, she can be a bit cranky at times and her special requests are stupid. (Whoever heard of buying a half head of lettuce!) They'll survive without her $50 a week. Too bad she's unhappy, but a big company like this can't twist itself into contortions just to save one little old lady from going down the street to the competition.

Sure, we believe in treating customers well, but we're business people. Let's look at the bottom line. After all, it can hardly be considered a major financial disaster to lose a customer like Mrs. Williams. Or can it?

The Cost of the Lost

The employees at Happy Jack's need to understand some economic facts of life. Successful businesses look long term. They look at the "ripple effects" of their service, not just at the immediate profit from an individual purchase.

The shortsighted employee sees Mrs. Williams as a small customer dealing with a big company. Let's change that view: look at the situation from another, broader perspective.

Ho, Hum, Just the Loss of One Small Customer . . . Or Is It?

The loss of Mrs. Williams is not, of course, a $50 loss. It's much, much more. She was a $50-a-week buyer. That's $2,600 a year or $26,000 over a decade. Perhaps she would shop at Happy Jack's for a lifetime, but we'll use the more conservative ten-year figure for illustration.

Studies show that *an upset customer tells on average between ten and twenty other people about an unhappy experience.* Some people will tell many more, but let's stay conservative and assume that Mrs. Williams told eleven. The same studies say that these eleven *may tell an average of five others each.* This could be getting serious!

How many people are likely to hear the bad news about Happy Jack's? Look at the math:

Mrs. Williams		1 person
tells eleven others		+11 people
who tell five each		+55 people
Total who heard	=	67 people

Are all 67 of these people going to rebel against Happy Jacks? Probably not. Let's assume that of these 67 customers or potential customers, only one-quarter of them decide not to shop at Happy Jack's. Twenty-five percent of 67 (rounded) is 17.

Assuming that these 17 people would also be $50-a-week shoppers, Happy Jack's stands to lose $44,200 a year, or $442,000 in a decade because Mrs. Williams was upset when she left the store. Somehow giving her that half head of lettuce doesn't sound so stupid when you think of it that way.

Although these numbers are starting to get alarming, they are still conservative. In many parts of the country, a typical supermarket customer actually spends about $100 a week, so losing a different customer could quickly double these figures.

How Much Will it Cost to Replace These Customers?

Customer service research says that *it costs about five to six times as much to attract a new customer* (mostly advertising and promotion costs) than it does to keep an existing one (where costs may include giving refunds, offering samples, replacing merchandise, or giving a half head of lettuce). One report put these figures at about $19 to keep a customer happy versus $118 to get a new buyer into the store.

Replacing lost customers can cost plenty.

Again, some quick math shows the real cost of the lost Mrs. Williams:

- Cost of keeping Mrs. Williams happy $19
- Cost of attracting 17 new customers $2006

Now let's make our economic "facts of life" even more meaningful to each employee.

How the Lost Customer Can Mean a Lost Job

The Robert Half Organization, a well-known personnel consulting firm, shows a simple way to calculate the amount of sales needed to pay employee salaries. Assuming that a company pays 50 percent in taxes and earns a profit of 5 percent after taxes, Table 1-1 shows how much must be sold to pay each employee (in three different salary levels) and maintain current profit levels:

Table 1-1 Sales Needed to Sustain a Job

Salary	Benefits	After Tax Cost	Sales Needed
$25,000	$11,500	$18,250	$365,000
$15,000	$6,900	$10,950	$219,000
$10,000	$4,600	$7,300	$146,000

These figures will vary, of course. But the impact on one's job can be clearly shown. If a $10,000-a-year part-time clerk irritates as few as three or four customers *in a year,* the ripple effects can quickly exceed the amount of sales needed to maintain that job! Unfortunately, many organizations have employees who irritate three or four customers *a day!* Ouch.

Self-Analysis

Applying the Mrs. Williams Example to Your Company

Let's take a few moments and go back to the Mrs. Williams example, but instead use your own organization. Suppose that you lose one customer and the other statistics hold true. Take a few moments to calculate the numbers as they apply to your organization. If you work for a non-profit or government agency where the dollar sales is not a relevant measure, calculate the number of people who may be aggravated or upset with you and your organization. Think in terms of the psychological price that must be paid as you deal with frustrated, angry, upset patrons on a day-to-day basis.

Calculating the Cost of Your Lost Customer*

A. Average or typical dollar amount
    spent (per week or month as appropriate): $_____ (per customer)

B. Annual dollar amount (weekly figure x
    52 or monthly figure x 12): $_____

C. Decade dollar amount (B x 10): $_____

D. Ripple effect costs (B x 17—people
    who may follow an unhappy customer
    out the door):   + $_____

Annual revenue lost: = $_____

Then,

E. Add customer replacement costs
    of 17 customers x $118 (a typical
    figure):   = $2,006.00

F. Minus the cost of keeping your
    present customer happy ($19 is a
    typical figure):   — $ 19.00

G. "Replacement" costs (E minus F):   = $1,987.00

Finally,

Total the revenue lost figures (B or C + F)

    a rough cost of your loss: $_____

*Note: These calculations are designed only to get you thinking about the ripple effects of unhappy customers. Their mathematical precision is not guaranteed nor is it that important. The point is, lost customers cost a lot of money.

THE CUSTOMER IS ALWAYS RIGHT
AND OTHER BALONEY

Most people accept, or at least give lip service to the idea that "the customer is the boss;" that he or she is a king or queen (or at least a prince or princess!). They talk about the customer "always being right." They say that the customer is "our reason for existing" as an organization, *ad nauseam*. Yet despite these claims, how is the service given? Often, not great.

The real challenge lies in translating such slogans into actions that convey these feelings and beliefs *to the customer*. Even when leaders truly believe in the importance of customer service, they still face the difficulty of getting the customer contact people to do what customers want—even when the customer's request may be a bit unusual.

> One of the greatest challenges lies in translating slogans or good intentions into behaviors customers want.

PICKLES   BY BRIAN CRANE

Customer service is easy until the customer asks for something unusual.
© 1997, Washington Post Writers Group. Reprinted with permission.

The problem gets trickier when you realize that the lowest paid and least well-trained employees are often those who face the customer every day.

- A multi-million dollar fast food restaurant, for example, places its success squarely in the hands of the minimum-wage teenager taking the orders and delivering the food.
- The image of a huge financial institution is created in the mind of the customer by the entry-level teller who handles his day-to-day transactions.
- A multi-billion dollar government agency is judged largely by the receptionist who answers the phone or greets the customer, thus setting a tone for any transaction. (Many a criticism of the "government bureaucracy" can be traced to a receptionist "getting off on the wrong foot" with a patron.)

When you really buy into the value of the customer and somehow communicate that to each customer, you virtually guarantee your success.

When you supervise others, you need to "infect" them with your same positive attitudes and skills. That can be a challenge for leaders, something we'll talk more about in Chapter 6.

WHY SERVICE IS IMPORTANT TO YOU. YES, YOU!

Businesses benefit from good service—but suppose you don't own a business. As "just an employee," what can you gain from developing service skills?

The short answer is that customer service skills are the same skills that bring success and satisfaction to all aspects of life. The best reason for learning the process of customer satisfaction is that *it will make you feel better about your life and yourself.* Sure, there are solid business reasons as we've already discussed. But ultimately, the personal advantage can be even greater.

> Service skills are crucial for success at all organizational levels.

Based on 30 years of business and professional experience in a variety of organizations, I am absolutely certain that people who apply the kinds of skills discussed in this book are happier, more productive, more successful and, yes, wealthier than people who choose to ignore the power of customer service. Take that statement on faith for now, but as you study and apply the ideas in the remaining chapters of this book, you will see what I mean.

We all start out as "peons" in organizations. Yet from day-one we choose how much we want to give to that organization. The more we give, the more we get. That's a principle of life that has been proven true throughout time. The flip side—giving the least we can get away with—is simply unacceptable. Giving average or substandard service will be hazardous to your career health. Undistinguished service leads to extinguished customers.

> A commitment to using customer service skills ignites a growth process.

The person who makes a commitment to mastering the process of customer service will be light years ahead of one who fails to do so. Betsy Sanders, a Nordstrom retail executive says, "The nature of such a [personal] commitment is perhaps best represented by a helix, which curves back around on itself but always moves up as it comes around. Thus, wherever you are in the process, the principles of service leadership provided can be applied to your situation now and will also support your ongoing development."[6]

The Customer Service Helix

Service Snapshot

Burgers Supreme

Steve and Debby K. own an independent fast food restaurant called Burgers Supreme. For more than six years they have built up a loyal clientele, many of whom eat there almost every day. Not only do they buy lunch at Burgers Supreme, but they bring in friends and fellow workers. Some of the regulars are teased about obviously owning stock in the restaurant, although none do.

The menu is broad, covering dozens of sandwiches, salads, soups, desserts, and specialty foods like gyros, onion rings, and frozen yogurt. Everything is prepared fresh. But the loyalty goes far beyond good food and fair prices.

Almost every regular customer has had the unexpected surprise of having Steve, Debby, or one of their employees say, "This meal is on me" and refusing to accept a dime. Obviously, this doesn't happen every time you go in, but it does reflect the owner's way of recognizing customer loyalty. It also reflects their willingness to empower their employees to give something away now and then.

The counter help at Burgers Supreme learns from Debby's example to greet customers by name, smile, cheerfully fix any mistakes, and keep hustling to make sure the restaurant is clean, even during the busiest lunch hour.

Faced with tremendous competition from national chains like Wendy's, McDonalds, and others (who serve similar fare), Burgers Supreme eats their lunch, so to speak, with friendly, individual, personalized service. They don't just talk the talk of customer service. They walk the walk.

THE ULTIMATE GOAL: CUSTOMERS FOR LIFE

The ultimate goal of customer service is to create customer loyalty. Understanding loyalty—what makes your customer loyal and how to measure this—enables a company or person to improve customer-driven service quality. We'll talk more about this later in the book, but for now, it is important to understand what loyalty means.[7]

What Customer Loyalty Is Not

Customer loyalty is sometimes mistaken for:

- Customer satisfaction alone. Satisfaction is a necessary component but a customer may be satisfied today but not necessarily loyal to you in the future.

- A response to some trial offer or special incentive. You can't buy loyalty, you earn it.
- Large share of the market. You may have a large percentage of the customers for a particular product or service for reasons other than customer loyalty to you. Perhaps your competitors are poor or your current prices more attractive.
- Repeat buying alone. Some people buy as a result of habit, convenience, or price but would be quick to defect to an alternative.

What Customer Loyalty Is

Customer loyalty can better be understood as a composite of three important characteristics:

- It is driven by *overall satisfaction*. Low or erratic levels of satisfaction disqualify the company for earning customer loyalty.
- It involves a commitment on the part of the customer to make a sustained *investment in an ongoing relationship* with a company.
- It is reflected by a combination of attitudes and behaviors including
  - *repeat buying* (or the intention to do so as needed)
  - *willingness to recommend* the company to others, and
  - a commitment to the company demonstrated by a *resistance to switch* to a competitor.

We'll talk more about customer loyalty throughout the book including how to develop a "customer loyalty index" in Chapter 5. For now, let's agree that customer loyalty is the highest goal of our service efforts.

Another Look
A Great Harvest![8]

While most company owners say that word-of-mouth marketing is important to their business, few take it as seriously as Janene Centurione, who operates two Great Harvest Bread bakeries in Ann Arbor and Birmingham, Michigan. The $2.2 million business turns loyal customers into experts, enlisting them to spread the word about the company's gourmet bread.

Centurione and her 50 employees look for enthusiastic patrons who ask lots of questions about the bread and pastry products. Employees then ask those customers to sign a guest book, which automatically initiates them into a "bread zealot" club.

Aside from funds for an occasional newspaper advertisement, virtually all of Centurione's marketing budget is used to inform and reward the special customers. Each month she sends out to almost 7,000 people (about 20 percent of her clientele) postcards that share information, like bread recipes. Zealots receive early notices about new product releases, along with the occasional 10%-off coupon. Some postcards thank customers for their referrals, which Centurione knows they're making, since the only place she mentions her latest breads is on the postcards, and the majority of orders come from people who say they heard about them from a friend.

Centurione estimates that the annual cost of keeping customers in the know comes to about $7 a head and that each recruit to the club brings in about $200 a year. She contrasts that with the $80 a year she spent on bringing in each new customer when she relied solely on traditional advertising. In two years, per-visit sales have climbed from $4.75 to $8.75, which she believes is directly attributable to an increased awareness of her products. Simultaneously, net sales have grown 18 percent a year for the past three years, while the number of zealots has increased almost 10-fold.

Probes . . .

1. Why do you think these customers become "enthusiastic patrons"?
2. How could your business apply a process like this to build customer loyalty?

A FINAL THOUGHT

Customer service skill development provides the most significant arena for career success. Whether you work for a huge corporation or you run a lemonade stand, the principles of customer service remain the same. You live and die by what your customers think of you.

In fact, *your number-one task*, regardless of your job title, organizational position, experience, or seniority will *always* be to attract, satisfy, and preserve loyal customers.

-------------------- *Summary of Key Ideas* --------------------

◗ No business or individual can succeed without creating customer satisfaction.

◗ Customers may be called by many names but all are engaged in an exchange of value. Some customer relationships are more intimate and complex but the exchange element remains constant. Moving customers toward deeper relationships with you requires service skills.

◆ Advertising is generally less cost effective in getting new customers than is word-of-mouth recommendation from an existing satisfied customer.

◆ The cost of lost customers can be many times the simple reduction of their sales. Ripple effects expand the loss dramatically.

◆ While all companies say the customer's satisfaction is paramount, few successfully translate good intentions into a workable strategy or specific behavior.

◆ Ultimately, service skills provide a master key to career and personal success. A commit ment to such skill development pays enormous dividends.

Application Activity

Interview a Service Provider

1. Interview five people about their customer service attitudes. Specifically, ask them to describe their internal and external customers and what they feel about the importance of serving them.

2. Ask two business people to estimate the typical amount customers spend with them. Then calculate the "cost of the lost" scenario like the one in this chapter. Ask the business person to react to this estimate. Does it seem plausible? Too high? Too low?

3. Describe three businesses that have won your customer loyalty— places you enjoy doing business and are likely to remain a customer with. What, specifically, causes you to give them your loyalty? (Note: Often it's subtle little things that win you over.)

4. What major corporations that you've heard of seem to be doing the best job of building customer loyalty? In what ways do they attempt to build long-term relationships with customers?

NOTES

[1] Berry, L. author of *On Great Service: A Framework for Action* as quoted in *The Seattle Times*, published via America Online, April 3, 1995.

[2] Glen, P. *It's Not My Department* (New York: William Morrow, 1990), p. 15.

[3] Bell, C. R., *Customers as Partners* (San Francisco: Berrett-Koehler Publishers, 1994), p. 5-6.

[4] Goldman, K. "Study Finds Ads Induce Few People to Buy," *Wall Street Journal*, October 17, 1995, p. B6.

[5] I first used this example in my book, Timm, P., *50 Powerful Ideas You Can Use to Keep Your Customers,* 2nd ed. (Hawthorne, NJ: Career Press, 1995), pp. 15-19.

[6] Sanders, B. *Fabled Service* (San Diego, CA: Pfeiffer & Company, 1995), p. xv.

[7] Adapted from a discussion by Purs, A. and Brandt, D.R.. "Understanding Your Customers," *Marketing Tools*, July/August 1995, pp. 10-11.

[8] Schafer, S. "Informing Customers," *INC Magazine*, June 1996. Transmitted on America Online, 6/18/96. Reprinted with permission.

The Customer Keeps the Score
In the eye (and heart) of the beholder

Research by the Forum Corporation suggests that 70% of the customers lost by 13 big service and manufacturing companies [studied] had scooted because of a lack of attention from the front-line employees. It's an emotional tie, not mere satisfaction that brings the customer back.

— Tom Peters[1]

THE WAY IT IS . . .

A great way for a business to fall on its face is to assume that it knows exactly what the customer wants—without actually asking the customer. In the 1980s and early 1990s Volkswagen Corporation of America saw its sales drop by 90 percent from its 1970 high of over a half-million cars to less that 50,000 in 1993. What happened?

Much of VW's competitive advantage in subcompact cars evaporated when competitors (especially the Japanese manufacturers) engaged in extended conversations with their customers and used feedback received to develop appealing features. While VW engineers "knew the *right* way" to position a steering wheel, Japanese compacts offered adjustable tilt wheels. While VW was certain that its radios were "just fine," competitors responded to customer desires for multi-speaker stereo sound.

The result: Customers perceived VW as offering less value. By the early 90s Volkswagen of America was fighting for its life. Today it is going through a dramatic turnaround after having paid a terrible price for not staying current with customer expectations and wants. To stay on top, you've got to involve the customer in defining value.[2]

----------------------   *Learning Objectives*   ----------------------

When you have studied this chapter, you should be able to

1. Recognize that everyone has pet peeves about the service they receive. In most cases, these irritators are little things.

2. Explain how the cumulative impact of little customer irritators can be dramatic, as illustrated by the Kmart versus Wal-Mart example.

3. Categorize customer turnoffs as arising from value, systems, or people problems.

4. Recognize the challenge of getting people out of their "zone of indifference" and into the category of loyal customer.

5. Cite the two major steps needed to create customer loyalty.

6. Apply five tips for better listening when dealing with customer complaints.

7. Organize and conduct an effective focus group to assess customer expectations and wants.

8. Function as a "mystery shopper" to gather data about the kinds of service customers are really getting.

EVERYONE HAS PET PEEVES ABOUT SERVICE

Get a few people together and ask them to describe some pet peeves about their experiences as customers and you'll get an earful. Everyone can recall situations where they were treated poorly, or products that just didn't measure up.

I often begin customer service training sessions by having the group generate a list of gripes to get people to think about specifically irritating experiences. You may find it useful to articulate some of your pet peeves. Take a moment to make a list of *specific* things that turn you off when you are a customer.

Think about your "pet peeves" about customer service.

Self-Analysis

My Pet Peeves in Customer Service

Quickly list your top ten specific turnoffs. What kinds of things irritate you when you are a customer? Think about several customer contexts: retail, repair services, restaurants, government agencies, etc. Be as specific as possible about exactly what irritates you. Perhaps cite a specific example if that helps you express your idea.

1.

2.

3.

4.

5.

6.

7.

8.

9.

10.

A typical list of turn-offs generated in a training workshop will include things like rude or indifferent service, having to wait too long, poor quality work (especially on repair jobs), sale items not in stock, dirty restaurants, phone calls put on hold, employees lacking knowledge, high-pressure sales tactics, or the employee talking down to you.

> Everyone has examples of irritating experiences as customers.

LITTLE THINGS MEAN EVERYTHING

Service turnoffs are, more often than not, little things that eat away at us. Problems with shoddy products or poor quality work happen, of course, but it's the little things that are most likely to grind us down in everyday customer experiences.

We can typically buy almost any product we want from several different vendors. We can buy a television from an upscale department or furniture store, a discount store, an electronics shop, a catalog merchant, a consumer warehouse, or even via the Internet. What causes us to choose one over the other?

> Since most things can be purchased from one of several places, what factors determine where we will shop?

Price is a consideration for many consumers, of course, but what if the prices are about the same? In those cases (or for the non-price sensitive* buyer) we are likely to decide on the basis of little things. Perhaps we like (or strongly dislike) a store's advertising approach. Perhaps the location is convenient, the merchandise displays are attractive, the clerks are friendly and knowledgeable, or the selection and warranty offered is good.

Perhaps nowhere is the illustration of little things making big differences more evident than in the competition among the giant discount retailers. In the 1980s the discount giant Kmart Corporation surpassed Sears to become the world's largest retailer. Kmart's reign at the top was, however, short lived. In the early 1990s Wal-Mart passed Kmart for the number one spot. What's the difference between Kmart and Wal-Mart?

Think about that question. What is the difference between a Kmart and a Wal-Mart store? You could list a lot of similarities. In fact, Kmart and Wal-Mart stores are similar in size, locations, layouts, colors, display, merchandise sold, and prices, and many other characteristics. So, what accounted for the stagnant growth of Kmart and the stratospheric rise of Wal-Mart in the mid-1990s?

> Little things can account for huge competitive advantages.

A good case can be made for the little things Wal-Mart has implemented to improve customer service. In fact, when I ask participants in training sessions to identify things they *expect* from a Wal-Mart that are different than Kmart, they inevitably cite:

- The greeters at the door to welcome customers
- Employees wearing vests with name tags to help customers find things
- Cleaner floors, tidier parking lots, stores that don't smell like popcorn
- Quick checkouts staffed with friendly people who actually seem to like their jobs.

Price sensitivity refers to how important price is for the customer. A price-sensitive buyer will be motivated most by a bargain, while less price-sensitive buyers are willing to pay more to get what they want.

Notice how I prefaced this list: Identify things they *expect* . . . to be different. As we'll see later in the book, expectations can be more important than the reality. Some Kmart stores do a good job with all the things listed above. But customers don't typically *expect* those things from Kmart.

The results of these kinds of little things are astounding. When Wal-Mart first surpassed Kmart in the early 90s both retailers had sales of about $34 billion a year. Five years later the gap has become huge. Kmart continues to sell in the mid-$30 billion range. Wal-Mart sells over $100 billion. And they sell the same kinds of stuff for about the same prices via the same number of stores! Little things mean *everything* when it comes to customer loyalty.

Greeters can put a human face on a large company.
© 1997, Washington Post Writers Group. Reprinted with permission.

THREE CATEGORIES OF CUSTOMER TURNOFFS

To better understand customer turnoffs, I've collected thousands of responses about specific things that irritate people. Some categories became clear as I analyzed the responses with researcher Kristen DeTienne. We found that customer turnoffs fall into three categories: value, systems, and people.[4]

Value Turnoffs

A fundamental customer turnoff is the feeling that they receive poor value in a product or service received. In short, shoddy products or sloppy work can send customers through the roof.

Value can be defined simply as *quality relative to price paid.* If you purchase an inexpensive, throw-away item at a discount store—say a 79-cent pen— you may not be upset if it doesn't last very long. But buy a $79 ball fountain pen that leaks in your shirt pocket and you're furious. If you make a major purchase of an automobile, an appliance, or professional service, and it quits working or fails to meet your needs, you will experience a value turnoff.

> Value is a function of product quality relative to its price.

The major responsibility for providing customers with appropriate value lies with the top leadership of the organization. It's the executive decision makers in a company who determine the products or services that will be sold. Value can also go back to the designers of the products (as in our opening story about Volkswagen). In a one-person enterprise, the owner determines the quality/pricing formula which defines value. If you run a lemonade stand, you determine how many lemons and how much sugar you will use. (Hopefully, you check with your customers to see how they like it.) Other people in an organization can affect value, but leadership bears the major responsibility for assuring it.

Systems Turnoffs

Say the word *systems* and many people think of computers. The term "systems," however, is broader than that. It is here used to describe any *process, procedure, or policy used to "deliver" the product or service to the customer.* Systems are the way we get the value to the customer. When seen this way, systems will include such things as

- Company location, layout, parking facilities, phone lines
- Employee training and staffing

- Record keeping (including computer systems for handling customer transactions)
- Policies regarding guarantees, returns, etc.
- Delivery or pick-up services
- Marketing and sales policies
- Customer follow-up procedures, etc.

> Systems involve any action or procedure used to get the product or service to a customer. System problems are primarily the responsibility of management.

The elimination of system turnoffs is primarily the responsibility of managers in most organizations. This is because often system changes require spending money (e.g., for planning new locations, remodeling, adding staff and training, initiating delivery services, etc.). Nonmanagement employees can and should be involved in suggesting system changes however. Management can get some of its best change ideas from employees at all levels. (Ways to get ideas from employees are discussed in Chapter 9.)

How Important Are Systems?

Some people argue that the majority of customer service problems are systems related. Business consultant Michael Gerber believes that systems are the key to business success. He cites hamburger giant McDonald's as an example:

Gerber talks about the frustration of small business people who fail to learn this lesson. He describes working with a client named Murray, who was so tied up in the day-to-day work of his business that he failed to grow a successful company. Gerber calls this episode, "The Day I Fell in Love With McDonald's." Here is an excerpt from a brochure advertising Gerber's "The E- Myth Seminar:"[5]

> When my meeting with Murray ended, I was exhausted. I had pages of notes, hours of conversations swirling in my head, and a long drive home. I needed a few minutes to collect my thoughts. So, I pulled into a McDonald's to grab a bite and sort out my notes.
>
> Talk about being confused. I didn't know where to start with Murray and his company. He loved his product and his dreams for the future. But something was wrong. I just couldn't put my finger on it. . . . Then it hit me.
>
> Maybe it's fate, but that day was the first time I was in a McDonald's twice in the same day. Suddenly, from the corner of my eye, I watched a lady approach the counter, and the young girl who was serving asked if she could take her order. Nothing out of the ordinary. But there was something about what happened that caught my interest. It was both what she said and her manner of saying it.

I've been to McDonald's restaurants from coast-to-coast. And I've been served by males and females, young and old, and many different ethnic groups. But regardless of where I am, or who is serving me, two very interesting things happen to me each time. First, I feel comfortable, because I know what to expect. And second, because I know what to expect, I feel in control of my experience.

At that moment I knew the secret of the McDonald's success. Wow! What an amazing discovery. Instantly I could see that this secret can work in any business. . . . The essence of the secret is how they [sell] that's so wonderful. It's their system that makes it a success. The key is that they have a system for everything. Regardless of who is working on a shift, the entire staff is taught the system. . . . There is no indecision. No confusion. No hesitation. No sour faces. No frustrated looks. Everything works like a well-oiled machine.

Gerber's observations illustrate the importance of effective systems in any business. It is the systems that can create comfort for both employees and customers. Knowing what to do and how to do it comes, of course, from extensive training and careful design of the delivery systems. Failure to do these things results in many customer service turnoffs.

People Turnoffs

People turnoffs are almost always the result of communication problems. Employees who fail to communicate appropriately, both verbally (with words) and nonverbally (without words), can quickly irritate a customer. Some examples of people turnoffs are

- Failure to greet or even smile at a customer
- Inaccurate information given or lack of knowledge conveyed
- Talking to another employee or allowing telephone interruptions while ignoring a customer
- Rude or uncaring attitude (like our donut clerk in Chapter 1)
- High pressure sales tactics
- inappropriate, dirty, or sloppy appearance (of the employee or the work location)
- Any communicated message that causes the customer to feel uncomfortable.

> Communication turnoffs are often a result of employee ignorance of the kinds of "messages" employees are sending to customers.

Employees at all organizational levels can and often do create people turnoffs, often unconsciously. In most cases these turnoffs arise because people fail to understand how they come across to people. Everyone interested in having a successful career would be wise to become continuous students of communication. Even the most subtle or unconscious behaviors can communicate the wrong messages and result in lost customers.

People turnoffs occur when customers feel you don't care.

GETTING CUSTOMERS BEYOND THE "ZONE OF INDIFFERENCE"

Thinking about customer turnoffs is particularly important when we consider that the correlation between customer satisfaction and repeat business (loyalty) is rather tenuous. Even satisfied customers may be neutral toward their relationship with a business, and the littlest thing can push them over the edge toward dissatisfaction. Service can meet their needs adequately but fail to motivate their continuing loyalty. Just as motivation researcher Friedrick Herzberg et al.[6] discovered long ago, satisfied workers are not necessarily motivated workers. Likewise, satisfied customers cannot be assumed to be motivated repeat customers. A "zone of indifference" exists between the satisfied and the motivated. Things are okay, but there is little to tie the customer to us in the long run.

Actually, customers who are satisfied may be *inert*, not motivated. Their satisfaction simply means the *absence of dissatisfaction*, not the motivation to become a repeat customer. A zone of indifference lies between the dissatisfied and the motivated (See Figure 2-1).

The challenge, then is to get beyond satisfaction to *motivation*. This is best done by responding to customer perceptions and expectations. Let's consider what we can do if we have a customer who is on the "dissatisfied" side of the continuum—a customer who needs to be "recovered."

Dissatisfied — Satisfied — Motivated

Zone of
Indifference

Figure 2-1 The Satisfaction-Motivation Distinction

Despite the best efforts of customer-savvy people, problems inevitably will arise. Problem situations should not be viewed as tragic, but as opportunities to further solidify customer loyalty. Anyone can give good service when customers don't have special needs, but it is precisely when a need or problem arises that customer skills are put to the test.

> Customer problems should be viewed as loyalty-building opportunities.

Chapter 3 goes into detail about how to recover the unhappy customer. For now, you need to know that the payoff for recovering a potentially lost customer is actually an *increased* likelihood that he or she will be loyal to you and even more likely to be motivated, according to our model. It sounds strange, but studies have shown that a customer who encounters a problem with a company—and has that problem addressed promptly and effectively—will be even more likely to remain loyal than a customer who never had a problem. Ironically, even in cases where the customer's problem is not resolved 100 percent in his favor, the loyalty still increases.

> Addressing and attempting to resolve a customer problem earns the customer's loyalty—even if the attempted solution is not completely successful.

Just the fact that the problem was acknowledged and addressed seems to be the key variable in strengthening the customer relationship.

An interesting example of customer recovery occurred when Toyota Motors introduced the Lexus line of luxury cars. With much fanfare, Lexus burst on the scene as *the* standard of excellence in its market. Shortly after the product introduction, it became necessary to recall the vehicles for a design defect. Toyota was, of course, embarrassed but went through with the recall of thousands of new vehicles. But someone in the organization (an optimist, no doubt) saw this recall as an opportunity to showcase the excellent vehicle service the Lexus customer would be entitled to. One selling point of the new line of cars was that it would be professionally serviced by exceptional dealers. Various dealers took the opportunity to make lemonade out of this lemon by doing things like:

- Calling customers and arranging to pick up their car so they wouldn't have to take it to the dealership
- Arranging for loaner cars while the work was done
- Giving every service customer's car a thorough wash and wax job free
- Apologizing and making recompense by giving customers gifts ranging from a fresh rose to a $50 bill to make up for the inconvenience.

In short, Toyota/Lexus turned a potential embarrassment into a watershed opportunity to demonstrate their service excellence. Many Lexus customers cited that experience as the reason they continued to have their car serviced at the dealership even after the warranty expired.

LOYALTY COMES FROM CUSTOMER AWARENESS THAT SERVICE *IS* YOUR BUSINESS

Customer loyalty arises from companies that make service an integral part of their operating philosophy. The "service department" should be a redundancy. Every department exists only to serve its customers, internal and external. Nordstrom executive Betsy Sanders says, "As long as you seek to add an extra dynamic to your business [like time, energy, and resources to isolate service as some special program] the results will be disappointing. Service begins to be meaningful when it is an internal dynamic. This dynamic develops when you accept service as the underpinning of your enterprise, believing that without your customers, you would not exist."[7]

Service must be seen as the very essence of your business, not just a side function.

Customers are quick to see the depth of a company's commitment to service. The organization that distinguishes itself in the eyes of its customers is rare. Most companies have not made enough of an impression one way or another for their customers to even think about them, much less to share these thoughts with others.[8] That element of loyalty—recommending a company to others—is lost because of undistinguished service.

EARNING CUSTOMER LOYALTY

How can we help a customer step outside the zone of indifference and become a "raving fan" of our company? Two steps make sense;

1. Reduce or eliminate value, systems, and people turnoffs
2. Exceed customer expectations to create a positive awareness.

We'll talk a bit about the first of these in this chapter and go into depth about exceeding expectations in Chapters 4 and 5.

RECOGNIZING AND ELIMINATING YOUR CUSTOMERS' TURNOFFS

The first step in reducing or eliminating turnoffs is to recognize their existence. The three categories described earlier (value, systems, and people) provide a useful way of categorizing and recognizing who shoulders major responsibility for each. But how can we tell if we are turning off a customer?

> There is no substitute for putting yourself in your customer's shoes.

The short answer is to put yourself in the shoes of your customers. Objectively assess the way they are treated and compare this with how other companies may be treating them. As Yogi Berra said, "You can observe a lot by just watching." A systematic way of "watching" is particularly useful because it gives objective data. Five major ways of gathering data include listening, explorer groups, mystery shoppers, focus groups, and feedback forms.

LISTEN WITH MORE THAN YOUR EARS

Few people are really good listeners, but those who are gain a lot of good information. Some people mistakenly think that listening is a passive activity—something you "sit back" and do when you are not talking. Not so. Good listening requires active mental work.

> Good listening requires active metal effort.

When you do it well, people will open up and share important ideas with you. Pay attention to your talk-listen ratio. If you talk a lot more than you listen you could be turning off your customer or failing to get good ideas on how to improve.

To be a better listener, use these ideas:

- *Judge the content* of what people are saying, *not the way they are saying it*. Customers may not have the "right" words, but they know what they need better than anyone. Look past their tone of voice or their inability to articulate exactly what they want. Fish for clarification.
- *Hold your fire*. Don't jump to make judgments before your customer has finished talking. If he's upset, don't respond defensively. Just hear him out.
- *Work at listening*. Maintain eye contact and discipline yourself to listen to what is being said. Tune out those thoughts that get you thinking about something else.
- *Resist distractions and interruptions*. Make the customer the center of your attention.
- *Seek clarification* from customers so you fully understand their needs. Do this in a non-threatening way using sincere, open-ended questions. Don't interrogate, but do ask him or her to help you understand what they mean, if you are confused. (Often the words "help me to understand" can be an effective way to show your concern and get clarification.)

Use Explorer Groups

Exploration involves going to other businesses to see how they do things. When you hear about a great idea another business is using, send out an explorer group to scope it out. One supermarket known for exceptional service encourages employees to take a company van and rush to the scene of good service given by others. They take notes and discuss possible implementation in their store. Explorer groups need not be sent only to direct competitors; often totally unrelated businesses have great ideas you can use.

Another way to gather great data is to "explore" how your own organization is serving customers by being a customer. Call the company and listen to the impression created by the person answering the phone. Is this what your customer is hearing? How do you like it? Then visit other locations or areas in your own organization and see how you are treated.

Call your own company and see how you are treated.

Try "Mystery Shopping"

A variation on this explorer idea is the use of "mystery shoppers" who visit company locations posing as customers. Trained shoppers—usually provided by outside shopper services— look for specific behaviors or processes and report their results back to management and the employees who served them. For example, a friend of mine owned several barber shops. He developed a checklist of things he wanted each of his hair stylists, twelve in all, to do. They included such things as promptly greeting the customer with a smile, introducing himself by name, asking how they'd like their hair cut, looking directly at the customer as he answers, calling the customer by name, maintaining a clean work area, etc. He then recruited shoppers, gave them the money for the haircut and a checklist. Immediately after having their hair cut, the shopper left the shop, filled out the check sheet, and then returned to the shop to reward the stylist by giving a dollar tip for each item checked. The system gave immediate feedback and reinforced what management wanted its employees to do.

> Mystery shopping works best when it is used to reward employees, not to catch them doing things wrong.

Mystery shopping is best when it is systematically done and the results are used to reinforce positive employee behaviors rather than to catch them doing things wrong. Be certain to have a specific checklist so that each employee "shopped" will be measured with the same yardstick.

The activity at the end of this chapter will teach you how to be a mystery shopper.

Use Focus Groups

Focus groups have long been used for marketing research but they can also play an exceptionally important role in understanding customer perceptions and expectations. Although some marketing consultants may disagree with me, there's no great mystery to how focus groups work, and any intelligent person could run one effectively. Here is the procedure:

- Select a random sample of your customers or patrons to join with you in the focus group session. Don't pick just people you know or customers you like. You may, however, want to be sure they are among your better customers by qualifying them according to their influence or how much they spend with you. You can get customer names off their checks or credit cards of whatever other records you have.
- Formally invite the customers to participate, telling them when and where as well as how long the session will take. Let them know the reason: that you are attempting to better understand customer needs and how you can better be of service to them.
- Keep your focus group to about a dozen people. Ask customers to confirm their attendance but expect that some will not show up. Fifteen confirmed reservations will generally get you twelve actual participants. Follow up with phone calls to confirm attendance. (One supermarket I worked with was so excited about the focus groups that they invited 40 or 50 people every month! The problem, of course, is that

a group that large makes it hard for all people to be heard. Some people dominated the group while others, who had equally good ideas but were uncomfortable speaking before so many people, suppressed their ideas.)

- Reward focus group participants. Tell those invited that you will give them something for their participation. Retail stores may give focus group participants a gift certificate, a free dinner, or even cash. In marketing research, it's not uncommon to pay people $50 or more for a one-to-two-hour session.

> Keep focus groups diverse, about a dozen people, and comfortable.

To get the most from focus groups:

- Set the stage by having someone from top management moderate the group.
- Create an open atmosphere where participants will feel comfortable giving you all kinds of feedback. Be polite, open, encouraging, and receptive.
- Don't ever cut people off when they're making a critical comment, and do not, above all, be defensive of the way you're doing things now, when in the eyes of the customer it's not working.
- Keep any follow-up questions open-ended. Don't interrogate.
- As focus group members express compliments, these should be acknowledged and thanked. Then make a statement such as, "we're happy to hear that we are doing things you like, but our major purpose here is to identify ways that we can do a better job in meeting your needs. How can we do even better?"
- Limit the group to a predetermined amount of time. Typically a one-hour or (maximum) 90-minute session works best. Any longer than that and you start losing people's interest.
- Tape record the entire focus group session and transcribe key notes for review. As you analyze the results of this group session, look for key words that might tip you off to what the customers are looking for. If, for example, concerns about the amount of time needed to complete their transaction comes up repeatedly, you might make the mental note to think about how you might meet customer needs more quickly.
- At the end of the focus group session, of course, be sure to thank the participants for all of their input—and give them their "pay."

Try Customer Feedback Cards

Many organizations solicit feedback via printed cards that customers can fill out and send back to management. While such cards can provide an outlet for customers and occasionally some useful data, several drawbacks are evident in many such systems:

Drawbacks of feedback card systems:

- Cards are generally competed only by people who are very satisfied or very dissatisfied. You get the comments on both extremes but less data from the middle—those customers who are somewhat neutral.
- Some cards ask the wrong questions. Designing the card calls for research skills to be sure you are getting valid data. I recall a restaurant feedback card that had a long list of yes-no response questions about food portion size, temperature, price, etc. I wanted to comment about the server but found nowhere on the card to do so.
- Occasionally cards require too much of the customer. While questionnaire formats can be too limiting, open ended cards may ask too much of a customer's ability to express himself. Believe it or not, I've also seen cards that require the customer to provide the postage.
- Sometimes the card fails to tell the customer what to do with it. Some can be submitted only in a dropbox in the store or restaurant.

Overall, feedback cards are less useful than the other methods of finding out about customer concerns. The apparent ease of having a feedback card system makes it attractive for companies too lazy to go after better data.

Service Snapshot

Monika's Attitude of Service

Monika L. works at a medium-sized Credit Union. In her two years there she has won repeated awards and bonuses for her effectiveness as a teller and member-services representative. Her supervisor consistently ranks Monika's work as outstanding and her opportunities in the financial service industry look rosy. When I asked her about her customer service "technique," she laughed and said she doesn't really have a technique, she just tries to treat people the way she'd want to be treated.

Monika pays attention to the little things, avoiding the people turnoffs as much as possible. When a member approaches her desk, she immediately looks up and says hello with a smile. If she's busy helping someone else, she at least makes eye contact to acknowledge the customer and let him know she'll be there to serve him in a moment. She is especially good at handling transactions quickly and efficiently without rushing the customer. When I asked her how she prepared for her career, she told me that when she was a little girl her favorite toy was a cash register. She loved to play store and keep Monopoly money in a special section in the cash drawer. She even used to iron her play money to keep it crisp, she laughed!

Technique aside, Monika projects a friendly, helpful attitude. She works hard to keep current on changes in systems and procedures and gives her employer 110 percent effort every day. She loves her job. Serving others with professionalism and skill is its own reward, she says.

Another Look

They Complain Because They Care[9]

Successfully resolving customer complaints can boost profits by increasing loyalty.

"When complaints are heard freely, deeply considered, and speedily reformed, then is the utmost bound of civil liberty attained that wise men look for." John Milton said that in 1644. More than 300 years later, smart retailers still pay heed to his words. In many ways, complaining customers are the best kind of business.

"It seems kind of funny, thinking about the complainer as someone who cares," says Amanda Prus, director of research and development for Cincinnati-based Burke Customer Satisfaction Associates. "But we found that if you're satisfied with a store, you're more likely to complain when something goes wrong." Complainers are likely to feel loyal to stores that trigger their outbursts, according to a Burke telephone survey of 1,179 randomly selected department-store shoppers. Furthermore, grousers are likely to remain loyal even after the incidents that displease them.

If this sounds similar to the tried-and-true parental motto: "I yell because I care," it's because the concept is the same. Parents yell because they have an enormous stake in raising their children. Shoppers often take the time to complain because they feel connected to a particular store. Rather than dumping it for another, they'll expend energy to try to make it perform the way they think it should.

Burke unearthed insights about complaining customers as a byproduct of an attempt to learn more about "secure customers"— those who feel great satisfaction with a store, would recommend it to others, and would shop there again. As it turns out, secure customers and complainers have similar profiles. Secure customers tend to be women aged 45 and older who shop at department stores at least once a month. Complainers are split evenly between men and women, but they are also likely to be older, frequent shoppers. In contrast, the most "vulnerable" customers are infrequent shoppers under age 35.

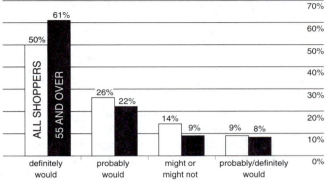

Determined Discontents

Older shoppers are more likely to voice their grievances.

(percent distribution of all adult department-store shoppers and those aged 55 and older by likelihood of reporting a problem to store management, 1995)

Source: Burke Customer Satisfaction Associates, Cincinnati, OH

Half of respondents say they definitely would report a problem to store management, and the likelihood of doing so increases greatly with age. Sixty-one percent of the 55-and-older set would complain, compared with 39 percent of those under age 35. Older people are also more likely to expect results, which may be part of the reason why they are willing to make the effort in the first place. Nearly half of older complainers but just one in five younger complainers expect stores to resolve problems satisfactorily.

Many of the people who say they would complain might not carry through, says Prus. Some don't want to spend the time, and others feel the time will be wasted. This makes the actual complaining customer a rare and special person indeed. JC Penney tries hard to accommodate and learn from such customers. In any of its 1,250 stores, "only the store manager has the final authority to say 'no'" to a customer's request for satisfaction, says corporate spokesman Hank Rusman.

Penney's also has discovered that its efforts in patching up disagreements go a long way toward strengthening customer loyalty. The Burke study confirms this notion. Shoppers who encounter problems and get stores to resolve them feel even better about the store than if things always go smoothly. "It's as if you were served a lousy meal at a restaurant, and the chef cooked you a whole new meal. That's what you'd remember and talk about," says Prus.

Cooking that extra meal is time-consuming, but worthwhile. Retailers and service providers of all shapes and sizes should think hard about how to handle malcontents, because they may see more of them in the future. Customer expectations are on the rise, and today's shoppers compare the treatment they receive not only from department store to department store, but from dentist to drug store to dry cleaner.

Burke Customer Satisfaction Associates incorporates the Secure Customer Index into most research for its clients; contact Amanda Prus at (513) 684-7607. For tips on how to turn complaints to advantage, see "The Sales Behind the Scowl" in the March/April 1996 issue of our sister publication, *Marketing Tools;* telephone (800) 828-1133.
—Tibbett L. Speer

A FINAL THOUGHT . . .

Moving customers from the zone of indifference where they may be reasonably satisfied into the category of motivated, loyal fans requires close and repeated checks of the ways we may be turning them off. This needs to be an ongoing process, not just an occasional set of actions. If we have made mistakes that leave the customer unhappy, we need to view this as an opportunity for solidifying a relationship with good recovery skills. We also need to continually seek information to direct the kinds of changes that will reduce value, systems, and people turnoffs. This is the first step to earning customer loyalty. The second step, exceeding customer expectations, is the topic of Chapter 4. But first, in Chapter 3 we'll look in more depth into ways to deal with the dissatisfied customer.

-------------------- *Summary of Key Ideas* --------------------

◆ Everyone has pet peeves about the ways they are served (or not served). These are often little things that have a cumulative effect in creating dissatisfaction or, minimally, an indifferent customer.

◆ The impact of a series of little things can have a dramatic effect on an organization's or an individual's success. These little things can work to our advantage or disadvantage.

◆ Customer turnoffs can be usefully categorized into value, systems, and people problems. Value and system problems are best addressed by company leaders; everyone can help eliminate people problems primarily through improving interpersonal skills.

◆ People turnoffs are almost always communication problems. Employees communicate inappropriate "messages" by their words or nonverbal actions.

◆ Value is a function of a product's quality relative to its cost.

◆ The term systems refers to anything involved with getting the product or service to the customer. It involves a wide range of procedures, policies, and systematic actions.

◆ Service recovery involves winning back customers when they have had a disappointing experience. A customer whose problem is addressed by the company will actually be more likely to do business with the company again than will the customer who never had a problem.

◗ Customer loyalty emerges when service *is* your business, not just an added dynamic. The term "service department" is redundant. All departments are in the service business first.

◗ We can best reduce customer turnoffs by listening to their concerns, using explorer groups to see what others are doing, using mystery shoppers to test our own service, conducting periodic focus groups to better understand what customers want or need now, and using feedback card systems..

◗ Although feedback cards are widely used, they often present drawbacks that contaminate the data received. These problems can be overcome with other data gathering approaches.

Application Activity

Let's Go Mystery Shopping

Select a minimum of four businesses of the same type (retailers, restaurants, banks, car dealers, whatever) to visit as a mystery shopper. Your task will be to pose as a potential shopper seeking information. You may want information about account types from a bank, details on a particular computer or appliance from electronics stores, information about a particular automobile, etc.

Be yourself during these visits. Don't attempt to act. Respond naturally to the employees. Don't go in with the attitude that you'll catch them doing something "wrong."

Immediately after each visit, complete an evaluation form. You may design your own form or use one like the sample below.

Sample Mystery Shopper Form

Name of business:_____   Date & time:_____

Employee's name _____   Task: _____
(if available)   (what you are shopping for)

                                                    Did / Did Not

A. When you entered, did the employee
1. Look up, make eye contact?   _____
2. Smile with a genuine smile?   _____
3. Acknowledge you with an appropriate greeting?   _____
4. Make you wait too long before helping you?   _____

B. While assisting you, did the employee
5. Project a positive, helpful attitude and
   willingness to assist?   _____

6. Pay full and undivided attention to you? _____

7. Deliver accurate and speedy, but unhurried service? _____

8. Ask you if there is anything else he/she can do for you? _____

C. Given the opportunity to offer or introduce other products, did the employee

9. Acknowledge or identify other things that may meet your needs? _____

10. Offer further information or introduce you to others for more info? _____

11. Ask you for your business? _____

D. When the transaction was over, did the employee

12. Thank you for coming in? _____

13. Invite you to come again? _____

14. Offer a friendly goodbye? _____

E. At any time during the transaction, did the employee

15. Ask for your name and/or call you by name? _____

16. Make you feel like a valued customer? _____

Score one point for each "did" answer. **Total:** _____

General comments or observations: What was particularly good or bad about the shopping experience?

Ground rules: Don't go in with a chip on your shoulder and don't overemphasize the negative. If you can't remember whether the employee did or did not do something positive, assume that he/she did.

When you have gathered your data from four or more locations, compile a brief report on what you found. If you owned this business, what would you do to improve the service? Be specific.

NOTES

[1] Peters, T., "Service or Perish," *Forbes ASAP,* December 4, 1995, p. 142.

[2] This story is covered in detail in "From Beetle to Bedraggled: Behind VW's Stunning U.S. Decline," *Advertising Age*, September 13, 1993.

[3] Excerpted from McGarvey, R., "Little Things Do Mean a Lot," *Reader's Digest.* June 1993, p. 33.

[4] DeTienne, K. and Timm, P., "How Well Do Businesses Predict Customer Turnoffs?: A Discrepancy Analysis," *Journal of Marketing Management* Vol. 5, No. 2, 1977.

[5] Excerpted from an advertising piece by Nightingale-Conant Corporation advertising M. Gerber's "The E-Myth Seminar" audiotape program. © Nightingale-Conant, 1996. This tape program can be purchased from N-C at 1-800-525-9000.

[6] Herzberg, F., Mausner, B., and Snyderman, B., *The Motivation to Work*, 2nd ed. (New York: Wiley, 1959).

[7] Sanders, B. *Fabled Service* (San Diego: Pfeiffer & Company, 1995), p.9.

[8] Ibid., p.3.

[9] Speer, T.L., "They Complain Because They Care," is reprinted from *American Demographics*, May 1996, pp. 13-14. Reprinted with permission of Dow-Jones Publishing and *American Demographics*.

Dealing with Dissatisfied Customers
Here's an opportunity for you

Those who enter to buy, support me. Those who come to flatter, please me. Those who complain, teach me how I may please others so that more will come. Those only hurt me who are displeased but do not complain. They refuse me permission to correct my errors and thus improve my service.

> — Retailing pioneer, Marshall Field

THE WAY IT IS ...

Successful handling of customer complaints can be a goldmine of repeat business. Some statistics from surveys reported by the U.S. Office of Consumer Affairs reveal some interesting facts. Among these:

1. One customer in four is dissatisfied with some aspect of a typical transaction.
2. A dissatisfied customer, on average, will complain to 12 other people about the company that provided poor service.
3. Only 5 percent of dissatisfied customers complain to the company. The vast "silent majority" would rather switch than fight. They take their business elsewhere.

But there is good news for companies that learn to effectively handle complaints. Such companies can charge an average of 8 percent to 15 percent more than their competitors, even in businesses where competition is keen. (Example: Maytag, the quality home appliance maker with the "lonely repairman" campaign supports a premium-priced product in a highly price-sensitive market.)

The best news of all is that customers who have their complaints handled well are very likely to do business with the company again. While only 9%-37% of dissatisfied customers who don't complain report a willingness to do business with the same company again, fully 50% to 80% of those whose complaints are fully resolved will consider doing repeat business—even if their complaints were not resolved in their favor![1]

We talked in Chapter 2 about the importance of reducing the turnoffs. These efforts are worthwhile but reality tells us that we cannot predict with certainty every possible customer complaint. In short, dissatisfaction happens. What we choose to do about it can make all the difference in creating customer loyalty.

> Customer recovery isn't always easy, but it is tremendously profitable.

This chapter looks at ways of handling the customer-recovery process. It's not always easy, but saving customers can be enormously profitable. Effective complaint-handling begins with the right attitudes coupled with the skills we'll discuss in this chapter.

-------------------- *Learning Objectives* --------------------

When you have studied this chapter you should be able to

1. Recognize the types of attitudes that can best lead to customer satisfaction and retention.

2. Apply the three step process to recovering the unhappy customer.

3. Recognize and be able to better deal with the chronic complainer.

4. Respond appropriately to a written complaint.

5. Apply the "3-F's" technique with its key terms, "feel, felt, found."

6. Recognize the difference between abrasiveness and assertiveness and apply assertiveness in appropriate ways when dealing with customers.

7. Understand the typical pattern followed by hostile or angry customers and know how to move the person toward "cooling off" and problem solution.

CUSTOMER RETENTION ATTITUDES

Hopefully, the discussion in Chapter One about the value of customers is firmly implanted in your mind. The best attitudes for service providers stem from the desire for a win-win relationship with the customer. Both parties want to feel good about the business transacted. This is not necessarily a "customer is always right" attitude. Restaurant owner Jeffery Mount explains:

> When I bought my restaurant, in 1981, I wanted it to become cutting edge: customer-centered, employee empowered, socially responsible. I read the business rags and listened to the gurus for the newest and the greatest teachings. Everywhere I went I heard businesspeople chant the mantra that the customer is always right.
>
> I even proudly hung on my wall that ubiquitous sign, which is plastered on walls of progressive companies throughout the land: *Rule #1: The customer is always right. Rule #2 If the customer is wrong, see rule #1.* I all but insisted that my staff pledge their allegiance to the infallible customer.
>
> My, how times have changed. There's no way you'll hear me say now that the customer is always right. We wouldn't be doing ourselves or our customers a favor by insisting on that.[2]

We'll come back to some examples from Mount's restaurant in a moment, but why do you think he changed his ideas about the customer being right? The answer lies in the fact that customers, just like you or me, at times make mistakes or demand unreasonable things. The oversimplified attitude about the customer's "rightness" is far less productive than one that says "I will do my best to provide the customer with satisfaction (and more!) whether the customer is right or wrong." What matters is an attitude of wanting to solve the problem at hand.

> The "rightness" or "wrongness" of a customer isn't the issue. What matters is wanting to solve customer problems.

Jeffery Mount illustrates with a story about a customer who was clearly wrong but who was treated in a manner that solved the problem, and built loyalty:

> Recently, a customer ordered finger sandwiches for a business luncheon. We advised against it. Wrong product, we warned her; too dainty, too small to feed hungry men and women at midday. Serve our hearty deli sandwiches, we suggested. "Oh, no," she replied. She insisted on finger sandwiches. Guess who called up, panicking, because "these sandwiches aren't going to be enough food"? "No problem," we said. We quickly created a bodacious big sandwich platter and delivered it in a New York minute. Even made a little money along the way.[3]

The issue was *not* whether the customer or the company was right. The attitude was one of cooperation and problem solving that won Mount's restaurant a loyal customer.

In addition to a problem-solving rather than blame-setting attitude, service recovery is best handled with an attitude of opportunity rather than in a manner that makes it appear a painful chore. Granted, most of us would prefer to not hear about customers' dissatisfaction. That's human nature.

Complaints are opportunities to cement relationships and create customer loyalty.

But given that dissatisfaction does occur, an attitude of accepting the opportunity and challenge can be useful. Customer complaints are opportunities to cement relationships. The vast majority of such relationships are worth saving, although occasionally—I stress *occasionally*—we need to let go of the chronic complainer, as we'll discuss later in this chapter.

Self-Analysis

What Are Your Feelings about Dealing with Difficult Customers?

Below is a list of words that may describe the ways you feel about dealing with upset customers. Select the five that most describe your general feelings. When you have finished this chapter, review these words to see if you have some better ideas on how to deal with these emotions. Discuss your results in a small group asking for feedback on how to deal with the feelings you have.

afraid	angry	anxious	apathetic	bored
calm	cautious	comfortable	confident	confused
contented	distraught	eager	ecstatic	elated
excited	foolish	frustrated	glad	hesitant
humiliated	joyful	nervous	proud	relieved
sad	silly	uncomfortable	uneasy	wishful

My top five: 1. _____ 2._____ 3._____ 4._____ 5._____

Recovery skills begin with the right attitudes(?)
© Tribune Media Services, Inc. All Rights Reserved. Reprinted with permission.

DEVELOP RECOVERY SKILLS

Customer service is easy when nothing goes wrong. However, a study by the Technical Assistance Research Program (TARP) estimates that approximately one in every four purchases results in some form of customer-problem experience.[4]

If you read the beginning of this book, you'll recognize the tremendous cost of losing a customer. Employees often underestimate the negative ripple effects caused by even one unhappy buyer. To reduce the impact of such ripples, we need to develop " recovery skills." As the name implies, we are here trying to recover the potentially lost customer. We can best do this by:

1. Feeling their Pain

The first step in developing such skills is to recognize that upset customers are likely to be disappointed, angry, frustrated or even in pain, and to blame you to some extent. Typically they want you to do some or all of the following:

- Listen to their concerns and take them seriously
- Understand their problems and the reasons they are upset
- Compensate them or provide restitution for the unsatisfactory product or service
- Share their sense of urgency; get their problems handled quickly
- Avoid further inconvenience to them
- Treat them with respect and empathy
- Have someone punished for the problems (sometimes)
- Assure the customers the problems will not happen again

2. Doing All You Can to Resolve the Problems

When attempting to recover an unhappy customer, the icing on the cake is the "something extra" you give by way of making up for the problem. Jeffery Mount's restaurant recovered the customer who ordered too little food by rushing in with the "bodacious sandwich platter." No matter that they tried to dissuade the customer from ordering the wrong food in the first place. They fixed it with something extra—a quick rescue.

Suppose you buy a new pair of shoes and the heel falls off. You call the shoe store and the owner says to bring them back and he'll replace them. You take time off from work, drive downtown to the store, battle for a parking space and spend about an hour doing this. He cheerfully gives you a new pair of shoes. Are you satisfied now?

Probably not. Why? Because he really hasn't repaid you for the inconvenience. Sure, he stood behind the product and perhaps even did so in a pleasant manner, but you still came out on the short end.

3. Going Beyond: Offering "Symbolic Atonement"

What kinds of things can we do to reconcile for the problem? Much of the remainder of this book will deal with this topic. Meanwhile, here are a few possible ideas that could be seen as going the extra mile in the eyes of a customer:

- *Offer to pick up or deliver* goods to be replaced or repaired. Lexus got a lot of mileage out of offering to pick up the recalled car rather than have the customer bring it in.
- *Give a gift* of merchandise to repay for the inconvenience. The gift may be small but the thought will be appreciated. Customer service expert Ron Zemke calls this "symbolic atonement." Things like a free dessert for the restaurant customer who endures slow service or extra copies of a print job to offset a minor delay are examples. It's the thought that counts.
- *Reimburse* for costs of returning merchandise such as parking fees, etc. (Many mail-order retailers pay all return postage fees to reduce customer annoyance and inconvenience.)
- *Acknowledge* the customer's inconvenience and thank him for giving you the opportunity to try to make it right. A sincere apology can go a long way. Make the wording of the apology sincere and personal. Say "I'm sorry you had to wait," rather than "The company regrets the delay." Empathy can be expressed with statements like, "I know how aggravating it can be to . . ." or "I hate when that happens and I'm sorry you had to go through . . ."
- *Follow up to see that the problem was handled.* Don't assume the customer's difficulty has been fixed unless you handled it yourself and have checked with the customer to see that the fix held up.

You may not have the authority to do all of these things (although many of these cost practically nothing) but you can go to bat for the customer with your boss. Just being the customer's advocate can help reduce much of the problem. If all goes well, you should feel a genuine sense of satisfaction after handling an unhappy or irate customer.

> If you don't have the authority to do what's needed to save the customer, become his or her advocate. Go to bat for the customer with your boss.

WHAT HAPPENS IF THE CUSTOMER IS STILL NOT SATISFIED?

Often you can creatively recover an unhappy customer, but this is not a perfect world and people are not always rational, so sometimes you too get upset. Professionalism requires that we do all possible to avoid letting our own anger or frustration reflect back on that customer or other customers.

The key things to remember are:

- If you *try your best to satisfy* the customer, you have done all that you can do.
- *Don't take it personally.* Upset people often say things they don't really mean. They are blowing off steam, venting frustration. If the problem was really your fault, resolve to learn from the experience and do better next time. If you had no control over the situation, do what you can, but don't bat your head against the wall.
- *Don't rehash the experience* with your co-workers or in your own mind. What's done is done. Recounting the experience with others probably won't make their day any better and rehashing it to yourself will just make you mad. You may, however, want to ask another person how they would have handled the situation.
- Use every customer contact experience as an *opportunity to improve* your professionalism. Even the most unpleasant encounter can teach useful lessons.

Look Back and Learn

When the customer situation has cooled, you may want to review with an eye toward improving your skills. Think back on the situation where you used your recovery skills and ask questions like these:

- What was the nature of the customer's complaint? Was it primarily value, systems, or people-generated?
- How did the customer see the problem? Who was to blame, what irritated him most, why was he angry or frustrated?
- How did you see the problem? Was the customer partially to blame?
- What did you say to the customer that helped the situation?
- What did you say that seemed to aggravate the situation?
- How did you show your concern to the customer?
- What would you do differently next time?
- Do you think this customer will do business with you again? Why or why not?

Review how you handled a situation with an eye toward improving your skills and professionalism.

Making careful notes of your responses to these questions can build your confidence and professionalism.

THE OCCASIONAL CUSTOMER FROM HELL

"Stubbornness is the energy of fools," says the German proverb. Sometimes we need to draw the line between upset customers with legitimate problems and chronic complainers who consume our time with unreasonable demands—the dreaded "customer from hell."

Be Sure This Really Is a Chronic Complainer

Step one in dealing with such people is to be sure you've got a chronic complainer. When you've tried the normal recovery approaches and nothing seems to work, look for the following telltale signs:[5]

- These customers always look for someone to blame. In their world there is no such thing as an accident: Someone is always at fault, and it's probably you.
- They never admit any degree of fault or responsibility. They see themselves as blameless and victims of the incompetence or malice of others.
- They have strong ideas about what others should do. They love to define other peoples' duties. If you hear a complaint phrased exclusively in terms of what other people always, never, must, or must not do, chances are you're talking to a chronic complainer.
- They complain at length. While normal complainers pause for breath every now and then, chronics seem able to inhale while saying the words, "and another thing . . ."

Occasionally we meet a chronic complainer.

What to Do with This Guy (or Gal)

When faced with that occasional chronic complainer (they really are quite rare, fortunately), try these techniques:

- Actively listen to identify the legitimate grievance beneath the endless griping. Rephrase the complainer's main points in your own words, even if you have to interrupt to do so. Say something like, "Excuse me, but do I understand you to say that the package didn't arrive on time and you feel frustrated and annoyed?"

- Establish the facts to reduce the complainer's tendency to exaggerate or overgeneralize. If he says he "tried calling all day but as usual you tried to avoid me," establish the actual number of times called and when.

- Resist the temptation to apologize, although that may seem to be the natural thing to do. Since the main thing the complainer is trying to do is fix blame—not solve problems—your apology will be seen as an open invitation to further blaming. Instead, ask questions like "Would an extended warranty solve your problem?" or "When would be the best time for me to call you back with that information?"

- Force the complainer to pose solutions to the problem, especially if he doesn't seem to like your ideas. Also, try putting a time limit on the conversation by saying something like "I have to talk with someone in 10 minutes. What sort of action plan can we work out in that time?" The object of this is to get him away from whining and into a problem-solving mode.

There are, of course, no guarantees when dealing with such customers, but the effort may well be worth it. Converting one of these folks into a normal, rational customer can be professionally rewarding. If it doesn't work, so be it. You've given your best and that's all anyone can ask.

> Get the chronic complainer to pose possible solutions to the problem rather than just dwell on blaming someone.

A Prentice-Hall booklet called *The Customer Service Manager's Handbook of People Power Strategies* includes the following section called "10 'Buzz Phrases' That Help You Disarm Irate Customers." Commit these to memory, use them frequently until they become comfortable and just roll off your tongue, and see how they can dramatically enhance your success with people in conflict situations.

Some useful "buzz phrases" when dealing with upset customers:[6]

1. **"Anyone in your position . . ."** The suggestion here is that the customer holds an important job or social rank. Don't be afraid to lard it on. No one ever gets tired of being told how good they look or how important they are.

2. **"I'd sure appreciate it if . . ."** This phrase implicitly asks the customer's permission, suggesting that the customer has the power to grant or refuse.

3. **"You could really help me by . . ."** Suggests that the customer is

not only taking a hand in the complaint-resolution process, but is also taking something of a parental or "older brother" role.

4. **"Perhaps you could give me some advice . . ."** Makes the customer into a veritable fount of wisdom.

5. **"Because of your specialized knowledge . . ."** Suggests a high degree of skill or advanced study. People love to think that others view them as highly intelligent.

6. **"Someone of your attainments . . ."** Suggests that the customer is a great success in life.

7. **"As you, of course, know . . ."** Suggests vast learning. This phrase is especially effective when you are telling customers something you know that they don't know. Most people don't like to admit that they are ignorant, even of things that they have no reason to know.

8. **"You're absolutely right about that . . ."** A routine but effective "stroke." Use it to readily concede some minor point the customer makes. The customer will then be more willing to give ground on the major points of contention.

9. **"Someone as busy as you are . . ."** Implies that the customer is one of the world's movers and shakers. Also suggests that the problem will be resolved as quickly as possible.

10. **"I'd sure be grateful if . . ."** Suggests an easy way to make someone happy, a natural human drive.

Note that some of these phrases start with "I," a word you should normally avoid in confrontations with customers. You can use it safely here because you are using "I" in a totally nonchallenging way. If you are feeling more aggressive, however, and a more confrontational approach seems to be in order, just start your remarks with the word "You."

HANDLING A NASTY LETTER (AND AVOIDING ONE OF YOUR OWN)

Customers don't write very often with so many other media like toll-free telephone "customer hot lines" available to them today. Nevertheless, or perhaps because they are fairly rare, a letter carries considerable impact. Letters provide a graphic and tangible reminder of a customer's dissatisfaction and have a nasty habit of appearing in your personnel file. So it makes sense to respond to them and to document what you've done.

If you choose to respond to a letter with a phone call, be certain to have the letter before you and to refer to the specific points as written. Also, make notes of what the customer says and how you respond. If you answer a letter with a letter of your own, be certain that the letter conveys your attitude of problem solving and projects goodwill and professionalism.

Written Communication Tips[7]

To be effective communicators, writers need to apply the same human-relations skills they would use in a face-to-face encounter. Specifically, writers need to be especially sensitive to people's feelings, interests, wants, and needs. Failure to do so creates unnecessary strains on relationships. The ability to get along with others, even on paper, is essential in a successful business career.

> Apply the same human-relations skills to your writing that you do in conversations.

Service Snapshot

The 3 F's: Feel, Felt, Found[8]

Seminar leader and author Rebecca Morgan teaches people how to express ideas so that upset customers won't become more upset. She describes the "3 F's" technique:

> The 3 F's are a skeleton on which to hang the rest of your response to a customer.
>
> This technique acknowledges the customer's feelings and offers an explanation in a way she can listen to. For example, "I understand how you could *feel* that way. Others have *felt* that way too. And then they *found*, after an explanation, that this policy actually protects them, so it made sense."
>
> Try using the 3 F's approach as she does. Be careful how you word it. Do not say "I know how you feel" (you really can't know exactly how another person feels) but do say "I can understand how (or why) you'd feel that way."

Let's consider a few principles of human relations and how these might apply in written communication. The first and perhaps most basic principle is that . . .

> Human-relations skills can be conveyed with appropriate tone.

PEOPLE ARE STRONGLY INTERESTED IN THEMSELVES

It is the nature of the human being—and all other known creatures, for that matter—to be concerned with and motivated by their own personal needs, wants, and interests. This self-centeredness, or egocentricity, is normal and not particularly harmful unless carried to the extreme, when there is *no* caring about others.

When people speak or write, they reflect this egocentricity in their language. A study once conducted at a Midwestern university showed that every fifth word written or spoken by a human being is *I* or one of its derivations—*me, mine, my, we, ours, us.*[9]

> Our primary motivation is self-interest.

Even though we are all self-centered to some degree, most of us learn to temper the tendency to focus on and talk about ourselves exclusively. Indeed, the extremely egocentric person is avoided like someone with a contagious disease.

> You can turn a person's natural egocentricity into an advantage by recognizing his or her needs.

The point here is that business writers can turn this egocentricity into an advantage if they recognize the reader's needs. Effective communicators learn to express concern and appreciation for the views of others in letters, memos, reports, proposals, and other documents.

PEOPLE PREFER READER-CENTERED MESSAGES

One important way to reflect consideration for your reader is by phrasing your message in terms of reader viewpoint. Expressing appropriate reader viewpoint involves much more than just selecting certain key words. Genuine reader viewpoint causes a document's tone to reflect a sincere interest in the reader. Self-centered writers think of themselves first. Reader-oriented writers think of and convey their messages in terms of what the reader wants or needs to know.

> The reader-oriented writer thinks of the reader first.

One "red flag" that the writer should look for is the words *I, me, my,* and so forth, found in abundance in written messages. Second or third person (you, or the impersonal, one) often conveys more reader-interest and objectivity.

Please don't conclude that you should try to eliminate the use of *I* and its variations. To do so may be impossible in some cases. In other cases, your efforts may result in rather tortured syntax and excessive wordiness. Besides, the use of *I, we,* or *me* does not always indicate a lack of reader viewpoint. For example, the person who says, "I hope you will be happy with this decision," is not really violating a reader viewpoint even though the sentence begins with the word *I.* The overall tone and sense of caring for the reader is far more important than simply avoiding the use of first-person pronouns.

Look at the following sample sentences and see the difference in the tone of the reader-oriented version compared to the "I-centered" one:

I-Centered	Reader Viewpoint
I'm applying for this job because it would give me some great business experience.	Since you are looking for a person who can step right into the job, I think you'll be interested in my qualifications which I feel could benefit your company.
I have received your explanation of October 23.	Thank you for your explanation of October 23.
We require that you sign the sales slip before we charge this purchase to your account.	For your protection, we charge your account only after you have signed the sales slip.
I have been a sales professional for 22 years.	My 22 years' experience as a sales professional provides a strong background in understanding customer concerns.
I am sending this software back to you for an update.	So that you may update this software with the most current version, it is being returned to you.
I'd like to show you my life insurance plan.	As a young father, you'll be interested in a life insurance plan tailored to the couple with small children and a limited budget.
We are happy to announce that we now offer a 24-hour teller machine.	Now you can bank with us conveniently with a 24-hour teller machine.

Phrasing ideas in terms of the reader's viewpoint conveys an interest in your reader and recognizes a principle of good human relations. Another principle of human relations is that . . .

PEOPLE WANT TO BE TREATED AS INDIVIDUALS

We can improve the tone of written documents by phrasing our information as though talking to individuals, rather than groups. A personally addressed business letter singles out a reader for individual attention. Such a letter conveys a more sincere regard for the specific person than one addressed to "Dear Customer" or "Dear Fellow Employee."

> The sweetest sound to most people is the sound of their own names.

Names or other information can be easily inserted while most of the letter remains the same for all readers. Explore these possibilities when you consider developing form letters to deal with recurrent situations.

Avoid the "Blanket Tone"

When a document makes the reader feel lost in the crowd, the "blanket tone" is responsible. For example, consider the blanket tone in the excerpts from letters below:

Blanket Tone	Personal Tone
When a thousand requests are received from prospective customers, we feel pleased. These requests show that our product is well received.	A copy of the booklet you requested is being sent to you today. Thank you for requesting it.
The cooperation of our charge customers in paying their accounts is appreciated. By paying on time, they allow us to give better service.	I certainly appreciate your paying the account. Your prompt payment allows us to give you better service.

> The blanket tone makes the reader feel lost in the crowd.

Address Your Reader Directly

Strive to express ideas in terms of the individual reader's benefit. One way to do this is through direct address. Here, the writer makes "this means you!" - type statements. Each day we see examples of this approach in television and radio commercials. The announcer "personally" addresses each of the several million people who may be listening and attempts to make them feel that they are spoken to as individuals. Direct address shows your readers how your message applies to them and how it can meet their individual needs in some way.

PEOPLE PREFER POSITIVE INFORMATION

Positive language often conveys more information than does negative language. It also tends to be more upbeat with a more pleasant tone. Rather than telling a person what is *not* or what you *cannot* do, focus on the positive—what *is* or what you *can* do. If you say "I can*not* give cash refunds on sale merchandise," it conveys only some negative information. It does not say what you can do; it only rules out one of the possibilities. On the other hand, the positive statement, "I can arrange to have the product exchanged for another model that may better meet your needs" conveys more specific and positive information.

Positive language also has a more pleasant ring to the ear. Yet many common negative phrases still creep into business writing. For example:

We *regret* to inform you that we cannot. . .

We have received your claim. . . [claim has a negative ring for most people]

Your *failure* to comply. . .

We *regret* that we cannot permit. . .

To illustrate the difference in tone between positive and negative word choices, here is an example: A corporate executive had to write to a local civic group denying a request to use the company's meeting facilities. To soften the refusal, however, the executive decided to let the group use a conference room, which might be somewhat small for its purpose, but was probably better than no room at all. Unfortunately, the executive was not sensitive to the effects of negative wording. She wrote:

We *regret* to inform you that we *cannot* permit you to use our clubhouse for your meeting, as the Ladies' Book Club asked for it first. We can however, let you use our conference room; but it seats *only* 25.

Review of the word connotations clearly brings out the negative words (italicized) first, while the otherwise positive message (you can use the conference room) is drowned out.

Had the writer searched for more positive ways of covering the same situation, she might have written this tactful response:

As the Ladies' Book Club has reserved the clubhouse for Saturday, we can offer you the use of our conference room, which seats 25.

No negative words appear in this version. Both approaches yield the letter's primary objective of denying the request and offering an alternative, but the positive wording does the better job of building and maintaining goodwill for the company.

Let's look at some examples of negative and positive sentences. Listen to the tone of each. (The negative words are in italics.)

Negative Wording	**Positive Wording**
You *failed* to give us the part number of the muffler you ordered.	So that we may get you the muffler you want, will you please check your part number on the enclosed card?
Smoking is *not* permitted anywhere except in the lobby.	Smoking is permitted in the lobby only.

You were *wrong* in your conclusion, for paragraph three of our agreement clearly states . . .	You will agree after reading paragraph three of our agreement that . . .
We *regret* to inform you that we must *deny* your request for credit.	For the time being, we can serve you only on a cash basis.
We *cannot* deliver your order until next Wednesday.	We can deliver your order on Wednesday.

PEOPLE DON'T LIKE ABRASIVE PEOPLE

If you tend to have a somewhat abrasive personality, it will come across in your writing and can hurt the tone of your message. Abrasiveness refers to an irritating manner or tone, the kind of writing or speaking that sounds pushy or critical. To determine if you tend to have an abrasive personality, you might ask yourself questions such as these:

- Are you often critical of others? When you supervise others, do you speak of "straightening them out" or "whipping them into shape"?
- Do you have a strong need to be in control? Must you have almost everything cleared with you?
- Are you quick to rise to the attack, to challenge?
- Do you have a strong need to debate with others? Do your discussions often become arguments?
- Do you regard yourself as more competent than your peers? Does your behavior let others know that?

The abrasive personality will tend to communicate in a manner that can be irritating to others. Try to recognize in yourself the degree to which you have a strong need to control or dominate other people. If you suspect that you do have this need, it would be important for you to make an extra effort to soften the tone of your written communications.

Keep in mind that there is a major difference between being abrasive and being assertive. Assertiveness simply means that you express your feelings and observations, normally phrased, in a manner that is non-threatening to other people. For example, instead of saying to someone, "You don't make any sense," the assertive person would say, "I'm having a difficult time understanding what you're saying." Or rather than saying, "Deadbeats like you burn me up," the assertive person might say, "People who consistently make late payments cause us a lot of extra work and lost revenue." Few people get offended by the assertive individual. Indeed, one definition of assertiveness is: "being pleasantly direct."

> Assertiveness and abrasiveness are different. To be assertive is to be pleasantly direct.

ASSERTIVE BEHAVIOR IS NOT AGGRESSIVE BEHAVIOR[10]

Many people confuse assertiveness with aggressiveness. Aggressive behaviors differ in the following ways:

Aggressors Communicate from a Position of Superiority. Aggressive people feel that they know best or must get their way at almost any cost. They see communication situations as win-lose, meaning that either they get their way or they have lost. And if they lose, someone else won! The idea of compromise or a decision whereby all parties benefit or win is foreign to them.

Aggressors Can Be Indirect, Manipulative, or Underhanded. The aggressive communicator may not be the guy or gal with the big mouth. Sometimes aggressive people use tricks and manipulation such as false emotion or acting false roles designed to get their way. (The TV detective Columbo is actually being aggressive in his questioning by playing dumb and getting people to reveal their guilt!)

Aggressors Set Themselves Up for Retaliation. Aggressive communicators eventually face adversaries. By being less than authentic, they spin webs of deception that get more and more confusing. Like habitaul liars, they eventually loose track of what they told whom.

Aggressors Use a Lot of Judgmental or Emotionally Charged Terms for Emphasis. The aggressive communicator thinks that strong language is clear but fails to see how it can create barriers to understanding. Emotional language almost always generates emotionally worded responses.

Assertive behaviors avoid these problems by being honest and authentic. They are based on beliefs such as the following:

High Self-Respect for One's Own Ideas and Abilities. Assertive communicators know that they are valuable. Their time, talents, and efforts are to be respected. They take a back seat to no one although they do recognize and respect other peoples' different abilities.

Respect for Other People. They see people as having a wide range of experiences and know that we can all learn something from another person. They know that organizational titles or social status do not guarantee people a right to the best ideas. People need people and can gain much from others.

Win-Win Solutions Can Be Found for Many Problems. The purpose of communication is to create understanding, not to beat out another person. Conflicts or challenges need not be couched as win-lose terms. A fresh perspective or creative twist can often be found to create solutions that leave no one as a loser.

Consensus Is Best Created by Direct and Honest Expression of Points of View. The assertive person wins by influencing, listening, and negotiating, not by manipulating.

Honest, Open Relationships Eliminate the Desire for Retaliation or Distrust. Communication does not get tangled in a web of game-playing. Openness begets openness. People are more comfortable with assertive communicators. They can be trusted.

Emotionally Charged Language Is Seldom Effective. Using strong, judgmental words hampers the resolution of problems or creation of understanding. Neutral, descriptive terms are better. They will not turn listeners off.

In addition to assertive and aggressive communication, some people are simply passive. They communicate ineffectively because they do not really care much—they are *apathetic*. Or they have chosen to stay out of a particular discussion. Do not confuse passiveness with assertiveness.

Another Look
Calming Hostile Customers[11]

A hostile, angry reaction usually follows a certain pattern if it is handled skillfully. This pattern is called the hostility curve. Here is what it looks like:

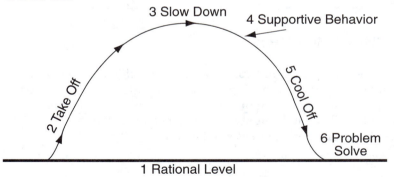

It is important to thoroughly understand each step of the hostility curve:

1. Most persons are reasonable much of the time. They function at a *rational level*. At this level, you can talk with them about things reasonably.

2. When irritations pile up or a specific incident provokes a person, he or she will *take off,* blowing off steam, possibly becoming abusive, and in general expressing a lot of hostility. Once the person leaves the rational level, there is no use trying to get the person to be "reasonable."

3. This takeoff cannot last forever. If not provoked any further, the hostile person just runs out of steam and begins to *slow down.* He or she may feel embarrassed for making a scene.

4. At this point, the staff member who has been listening to this hostile takeoff can say something. What you say makes a big difference. Say something *supportive,* such as "Things can be awfully frustrating when you're under so much pressure" or "I know this has been an upsetting experience for you." In addition, you must be supportive in your nonverbal behavior. Being supportive does not necessarily mean agreeing, but it does mean letting the other person know that you understand his or her feeling.

5. If you do say something supportive, you will usually see the hostile person *cool off.* He or she comes back down to the rational level.

6. Once the person has returned to the rational level, you can begin to *problem solve* with him or her about what caused the anger. Persons are in a mood to problem solve when they are rational, not when they are at the top of the hostility curve.

Probes . . .

1. Why is it important to help an upset customer cool off before trying to solve the problem?

2. How can you best help him or her through the hostility curve? What specific things could you say? What should you avoid saying or doing?

A FINAL THOUGHT

Customer complaints are opportunities for building customer loyalty. Sure, complainers can be annoying, but they can also be your best friend. They can point out ways to improve and strengthen your business in ways no one else will. That's valuable intelligence for the competitive battlefield. Use it to build customer satisfaction and loyalty.

Application Activity
Defusing and Recovering the Unhappy Customer[12]

Read the following brief case. Then get another person to role play the part of the unhappy customer. Practice responding to his or her concerns in a constructive manner that could lead to recovery of this customer. If possible, videotape your role play and review the tape to identify nonverbal and verbal behaviors.

Before you get into this activity, look carefully at the language used to describe the situation. What problems do you see about the tone? How could you express the viewpoints of the two parties in more constructive terms?

The Motel Manager's Story

A fellow from a city several hundred miles away has just checked into your motel. He gives the impression that he is a big-shot government worker. After a short visit to his room, he storms into your office, claiming his air conditioner is faulty. You have recently spent seventy-five dollars to repair the unit in his room. You are certain that he must have banged it with his fist and that he is responsible for the trouble with the unit. You are not about to let him push you around.

The Traveler's Story

You have just settled into a rather dumpy motel. It is mid-August, and the temperature is 109 degrees. You flip on the switch to the air conditioner; there is a buzz, a hum, and smoke starts to pour out of the vents of the air conditioner. After several bangs with your fist, the smoke vanishes, but the air conditioner will not work. You are hot and tired, and wish you had selected a finer motel. At that point, you storm into the motel manager's office, inform him that he mans a cheap, dumpy, and poorly cared for motel. You demand that he rush immediately to your room and repair your air conditioner.

------------------- *Summary of Key Ideas* -------------------

◗ Customer retention requires positive attitudes toward problem solving but not necessarily an oversimplified "customer is always right" mind set.

◗ The key issue in customer disputes is not who is right or who is wrong, but rather how can all parties cooperate to solve the customer's concerns.

◗ A customer complaint is an opportunity to cement a relationship and create customer loyalty.

◗ Recovery skills are necessary to career success and will be regularly used.

◗ The key skills in recovery involve feeling the customer's "pain," doing all you can to resolve the problem, and then going the extra step via "symbolic atonement."

◗ After doing your best to deal with a customer problem, it is useful to review the episode and learn from it.

◗ Handling the occasional chronic complainer can best be done by understanding his or her motives and then getting the complainer to propose an acceptable solution.

◆ Effective written communication uses human relations principles such as reader self- interest, reader-centeredness, and individual treatment using positive information.

◆ Abrasiveness is a drawback to customer relations while assertiveness leads to better problem resolution.

NOTES

[1] These Office of Consumer Affairs statistics were quoted in the *Customer Service Manager's Handbook of People Power Strategies* (Upper Saddle River, NJ: Prentice Hall, 1989), p.3.

[2] Mount, J., "Why Take Sides," *Inc.* March 1995, 17(3), p.29.

[3] *Ibid.*

[4] TARP research is cited in J. R. Shannon, "The Components of Customer Service: A New Taxonomy," *Journal of Customer Service in Marketing & Management*, Vol. 2(1), 1996, p. 6.

[5] Adapted from "How to Deal With Those Chronic Complainers," in *Customer Service Manager's Letter*, September 20, 1989. Published by Prentice Hall Professional Newsletters. The article is based on the work of Dr. Robert Bramson, *Coping With Difficult People* (New York: Dell, 1988).

[6] Excerpted from *Customer Service Manager's Handbook of People Power Strategies* (Upper Saddle River, NJ: Prentice Hall Professional Newsletters, 1989), pp. 9-10. Reprinted with permission.

[7] This material is adapted from Timm, P. and Stead, J., *Communication Skills for Business and Professions* (Upper Saddle River, NJ: Prentice Hall, 1996), Chapter 9.

[8] Morgan, R. L., Calming Upset Customers (Menlo Park, CA: Crisp Publications, 1989), p. 40.

[9] Daniel Starch, *How to Develop Your Executive Ability* (New York: Harper & Row, 1943), p. 154.

[10] Timm, P., *Basics of Oral Communication* (Cincinnati, OH: South-Western Publishing, 1993), pp. 237-38. Reprinted with permission of the publisher.

[11] Adapted from ideas presented in *Teaching Patient Relations in Hospitals: The Hows and Whys* (New York: The American Hospital Association, 1983).

[12] This case originally appears in Timm, P.R. and Peterson, B. D., *People at Work* (St. Paul, MN: West Educational Publishing, 1993) p. 263.

The Power of Expectations Exceeded

The master key called E-Plus

Customers have learned to expect quality products and services. What more must you give them?

THE WAY IT IS . . . BABY BOOMERS MAY SEEK AGE-FRIENDLY STORES[1]

Easier-to-read labels. Comfortable seating throughout stores. Well-lighted parking lots. Clerks knowledgeable about the merchandise.

Those are among the changes some experts forecast as retailers seek to accommodate an aging population, including a looming "mountain of middle age." By decade's end, people 35 to 54 years old will be the dominant and fastest-growing part of the U.S. population, with perhaps $280 billion more in spendable income than the segment had just two years ago.

But aging baby boomers may be hard-to-please consumers, says Stephen A. Taylor of Age Wave, an Emeryville, California firm that advises businesses on how to satisfy that maturing market. They not only will retain their expectations for quality in what they buy; as they move through middle age and their bodies slow down; they will also demand convenient shopping environments.

For retailers, that's likely to mean more rest stops in stores, shelving arranged so customers needn't bend over and bigger type on labels. Don't be surprised if some merchants attach magnifying glasses to shopping carts, Mr. Taylor says. Safety concerns may result in fewer free-standing displays around blind corners, while dimly lit parking lots will be a growing issue, the consultant recently told attendees at the Food Marketing Institute convention in Chicago.

"This is the best-educated generation in American history," Mr. Taylor says. "They are oriented toward finding out about what they're buying, what's in it, what's good for them." Thus, supermarkets may want to add in-store dietitians to answer consumers' questions.

But along with their increasing demands on retailers, the middle-aged consumers will spend more to satisfy their needs—a forecast that augurs well for upscale products, the consultant says. "As they get older people will say, 'We've lived this long, let's not cut corners.'"

-------------------- *Learning Objectives*   --------------------

When you have studied this chapter, you should be able to

1. Explain the psychological underpinnings that support the strategy of exceeding customer expectations to create retention and loyalty.

2. Understand how expectations of a core product and overall expectations of the entire customer experience are different.

3. Explain the acronym VISPAC as it applies to customer expectations.

4. Predict what kinds of actions will be likely to create an E-Plus experience.

5. Apply the power of VISPAC by using idea-generation sessions with employees.

As this opening story shows, people's needs, wants, and expectations change. Retailers and other businesses need to be vigilant in spotting such changes and adapting their businesses accordingly. Reacting to customer change is good, but being proactive in anticipating change is better.

How can you best anticipate changing customer needs? Staying close to the customer and maintaining an ongoing dialogue is an important key. But just what can you do with the input received from customers? You can use it to best understand their current expectations and, more importantly, to plan approaches that will exceed these expectations. Ultimately, today's customer service success arises from a central theme that is simple to state yet challenging to impliment. The underlying theme is:

> You achieve customer satisfaction, retention, and loyalty by exceeding customer expectations in positive ways.

We'll call this process of exceeding expectations *E-Plus*. Research and experience of countless experts points to E-Plus as almost a "master

> E-Plus is an approach supported by basic psychological theories. It utilizes human nature to create a win-win relationship.

key" to service success. Before we look at the E-Plus formula, and suggest some ways to successfully implement this approach, let's consider some background that can explain the psychology behind E-Plus.

WHY CUSTOMERS DO WHAT THEY DO

At a basic psychological level, people are motivated to act in a particular way because their action will either result in a gain (reward) or avoid a loss (punishment). Customers are rational people. If a buying experience is positive, they will see it as a gain and probably come back; if negative, they'll regard it as a loss and try to avoid returning. If it's so-so, they'll stay in that zone of indifference we discussed back in Chapter 2.

The Crucial Role of Customer Expectations

As customers entering into a transaction, they expect (albeit perhaps unconsciously) to be treated a particular way. What they expect is often based on their past associations with this business, person, organization, or ones they see as similar. If they had a good experience in the past, they'll probably expect something satisfactory. If the last transaction wasn't so positive, they might assume the next one won't be better.

The part of all this that frustrates customer service people is that expectations are *perceptual*. They exist in the mind of our customer. Some-

> As people enter into a transaction, they harbor certain expectations of how it will be.

times they are accurate and rational, sometimes they aren't. And to make matters worse, they are ever-changing (as we saw in the opening story about baby boomers). They present a moving, hard-to-define target.

Expectations of Products, Services, and the Customer Experience

When people judge the quality of a tangible product, they use fairly objective and somewhat predictable standards. For example, if a person buys a new automobile, they'll be likely to judge its quality by things like

- driving and handling characteristics
- low frequency of repair (it seldom has to be fixed)
- appropriate size (it holds my family comfortably)

- a good price relative to its quality (it looks nice but didn't cost an arm and a leg)
- workmanship (it seems to be well built, nice paint job).

Likewise when we judge the quality of a service (say a house painter's job) we measure it by such standards as

- the work was done on time (he met the deadline)
- the surfaces to be painted were carefully prepared
- the paints were mixed and applied neatly
- the painter cleaned up after the job, etc.

These kinds of standards are pretty predictable. They're much the same for each customer.

> Customer satisfaction goes beyond the core product. Customers evaluate the entire buying experience.

But evaluating the degree of customer satisfaction goes beyond the core product or service bought. It involves the entire buying experience. The standards by which customers measure satisfaction are more ambiguous.

Self-Analysis

Identifying Some Core Expectations

Identify your core expectations for the following products or services. What must happen for you to maintain a basic level of customer satisfaxction?

Purchase of:
A washing machine

A computer system

Repair of your automobile's transmission

Lawn service for your home

Copy service for an important report

A new bicycle

A dental check-up

A complete physical

Carpet cleaning.

Be specific about what you'd consider to be basic expectations.

Cutomers will be unhappy if their basic expectations are not met.

To further complicate matters, expectations will be different among different organizations or under differing circumstances. When purchasing a tangible product, people expect different treatment from a "high-touch," full-service retailer than they do from a warehouse store. They expect different service from a prestigious law firm than from a state auto license bureau.

For that matter, they probably expect something different from the same store at different times. Perhaps a little less personal attention is anticipated during busy periods (like Christmas shoppers or end-of-month license plate buyers).

Different Expectations from Different Businesses

Suppose you intend to shop at a low cost, self-service, discount store, like a Kmart, Target, or Fred Meyers. Going into the store, you expect to be treated in a particular way. You do not necessarily expect that the clerk in the clothing department (if you can find one) will be an expert in fitting clothing. Nor would you be likely to expect that person to be particularly helpful in choosing or color coordinating items we may want to purchase. This is not to say

> Our expectations differ with different types of businesses.

that some people who work there would not have these skills, but we probably wouldn't expect them as a general rule.

If we simply select some clothing items from a rack and take them to a checkout for purchase, we are not surprised nor particularly disappointed. That's about what we expected and if other aspects of the store are okay (it seems clean and well-stocked, for instance) we could be perfectly satisfied.

By contrast, if we were to go to a Nordstrom's, Macy's, or Bloomingdale's full-service department store, or to an expensive boutique, we would expect a different kind of transaction. We would probably expect to have a person working in a clothing department who has considerable expertise in clothing fit, color, and materials. We would realistically expect that service person to give us some attention and assistance as we make our purchases.

When we find situations like these just described, our expectations are met. Dissatisfaction is probably avoided; we are in that zone of indifference.

> When a customer finds his or her expectations exceeded, the likelihood of becoming a repeat customer increases sharply.

The key to exceptional customer satisfaction and a corresponding motivation to return (loyalty), however, lies not in meeting expectations but in *exceeding* them.

One of three situations may arise as we compare our expectations with the service received:

• Positive expectations not fulfilled (experience not as good as expected)	• Expectations met	• Negative expectations not fulfilled (experience not as bad as expected)
• Experience more negative than expected		• Experience more positive than expected

In the condition described in the left column, the customer's experience was as bad or worse than expected. She's dissatisfied and likely to defect to another provider, if she has a rational alternative. The middle column customer is neither dissatisfied nor particularly motivated to return. This is the zone of indifference we discussed earlier.

In the right column situation, the transaction was better than expected. Either the customer thought it would be pretty good and it was very good, or the customer thought it wouldn't be good but it wasn't as bad as expected. If positive expectations were sufficiently exceeded (or negative ones shown to be unfounded), this customer is a very good candidate for repeat business.

The right column situation is what we'll call an *E-Plus* experience—customer expectations were *exceeded*.

WHY E-PLUS LEADS TO CUSTOMER RETENTION

A solid theoretical basis for predicting that the E-Plus (right column) customer will become a repeat customer exists in a theory founded in social psychology called *Equity Theory*. Psychologist J. Stacy Adams first articulated this theory in the mid 1960s.[2] It has stood the test of time to be widely accepted as a predictor of some kinds of human behavior. Here is a quick summary of the theory:

> E-Plus is based in a theory from social psychology called equity theory.

Equity theory starts with the premise that human beings constantly go into and out of various kinds of relationships ranging from the intimate to the cursory. Long-term relationships like best friendships and family are on one end of the continuum. Brief, even momentary "relationships," like buying something from a convenience store on a cross-country trip or chatting with someone in an airport, are on the other end of the continuum. The buyer-seller relationship is germane to this discussion.

> We all constantly go into and out of relationships with other people. Some are lasting, some only momentary.

Once in a relationship, even a brief one, people immediately and regularly assess the *relative equity or fairness of their involvement* compared to other people. They check to see if what they give to the relationship balances with what they are getting out of it. A very simple example of a relationship that is out of balance (inequitable) would arise if you pass another person in the hallway or on the street and say hello to him but he ignores your greeting and walks on. You've given something and received nothing in return. You'll feel funny about this awkward state. A higher level experience might be if you invite a new friend and his family to your home for dinner and he never even thanks you, let alone invites you to his place for a meal. Common courtesy demands that he do something to "rebalance"

> People in relationships constantly monitor the relative fairness of the relationship. Are they getting as much from it as they are giving to it?

the relationship. Perhaps he could bring a gift, something to share at the meal, or the like. People who take but never give are soon found lonely.

Initially, much testing of this theory focused on the workplace where workers' perceptions of fairness (equity) were correlated with certain behaviors. Not surprisingly, studies found that people who were paid less for doing the same work as others, for example, felt a sense of inequity. In my own doctoral dissertation research, I found that employees who sensed that their supervisor communicated more often and more positively with other employees in the workgroup felt a clear sense of inequity.[3]

But the theory goes beyond simply citing situations where people may feel inequitably treated. It also predicts what people would do about it. When inequity is sensed, people will respond with one or some combination of the following:

- *Ignore or rationalize the inequity.* ("He deserves to be treated better than I," "The world isn't fair but I'm not going to fight it," or "I guess he didn't hear me say hello.")
- *Demand restitution.* (The offended person goes to the boss to demand a fairer pay, or the customer wants her money back when product quality is poor.)
- *Retaliation* (This can range from telling others about how bad the organization is, doing harm to the person seen as the cause of the inequity, to outright sabotage.)
- *Withdraw from the relationship.* (Quit and don't come back.)

So far this theory seems to bear out common sense. If we feel we are being unfairly treated, we get upset and usually do something about it. Hence, the unsatisfied participant in a relationship (the customer in our case) is likely to do one of these things. The first two alternatives may give you as a business a chance to patch things up and retain the customer, using techniques such as those learned in Chapter 3. But the last two—retaliation or withdrawal—can be devastating. Mrs. Williams, the former Happy Jacks Super Market customer in our Chapter 1 story, did both. She withdrew—quit shopping there—and retaliated by telling her friends, thus starting the negative ripple effects that may have resulted in scores or even hundreds of lost customers or potential customers.

THE POSITIVE SIDE OF EQUITY THEORY

Another finding of equity theory predicts this: People who feel that they are receiving *more than they "deserve"* from a transaction also experience a psychological need to restore the balance of fairness. A simple illustration of this is the social pressure you may feel to reciprocate when someone invites you to their home for dinner. The relationship will remain unbalanced until you rebalance it with a similar kindness: bringing wine or

> People who feel they are getting *more* from the relationship that they put in will also feel psychological pressure to restore a balance.

flowers, inviting them to your home, or at least sending a thank you note.

Herein lies the theoretical basis for exceeding customer expectations. By going beyond the expected, you are creating an imbalance that, for many people, will require action on their part to rebalance. The logical options are the opposite of what the victim of a negative imbalance feels: They could rationalize or ignore it, of course, but attempts to restore the balance could also take the form of telling others of the positive experience, paying a premium for the goods received, or, in short, becoming a loyal customer.

The challenge, then, is to *create positive imbalances by exceeding customer expectations.* This is the master key called E-Plus. Using this master key requires two kinds of ongoing actions:

1. Continually work to anticipate customer expectations, and then
2. exceed these expectations.

ANTICIPATING CUSTOMER EXPECTATIONS

Two ways to get a sharper picture of the customer's ever-changing expectations are by fishing for feedback and being receptive to customer input.

How to Fish for Feedback

Two of the best tools for the feedback fisher are "naive" listening and focus groups. Naive listening is more of an attitude than a strategy. As its name implies, this kind of listening conveys that you don't know—are naive—about what the customer wants. Your task is to get them to explain it to you. Create an atmosphere where you and your people are cheerfully receptive to customer comments—*especially* receptive—to comments that might not be so pleasant to hear.

> The best way to get useful feedback is to create an atmosphere where your customers can comfortably give suggestions or complain.

The best way to get feedback is to make it easy to complain. Let customers know that you are receptive to their problem or concerns. Then provide ways for them to tell you what's on their minds. The use of *open-ended* questions is particularly important. An open-ended question is one that cannot be answered with a simple yes or no or a one-word response. As such they invariably convey much more information. Restaurant servers who ask, "How else can I make your dinner enjoyable?" will get a broader range of responses than one who asks the more common, "Do you need anything else?" or "Is everything okay?"

Of course, questions aren't just for the complainer. We also need to know what changes we need to make to maintain our customers' ever-changing expectations. Here is where the focus group comes in. Review the material on focus groups in Chapter 2 if you've forgotten how these work.

Go fishing for feedback—regularly. Open up the communication channels and give your customer an opportunity to comment and complain. Recall, as we said earlier, at least 63 percent of unhappy customers who do not complain will defect to another source of products or services. Of those who do complain *and have their problems addressed, even if not fully resolved*, only 5 percent will abandon your business. In a sense, your complaining customer is your best customer. Meeting his or her needs provides an opportunity to solidify a business relationship.

> Your complaining customer is often your most valuable customer.

Understanding customer expectations will do little good unless you take the second step in the E-Plus process: regularly develop ways to exceed expectations.

EXCEEDING CUSTOMER EXPECTATIONS

Take a look at your responses to the exercise on page 64 where you identified some core expectations about several products or services. Now that you've identified the basics needed to keep you satisfied, what might be some unexpected surprises that you could receive from an enlightened business applying E-Plus? What kinds of little things could make you much more likely to become a loyal customer?

Now let's go back to our ficticious Kmart, Target, or Fred Meyers-type discount store. How might this retailer exceed your expectations—provide some level of service above and beyond what you'd normally expect?

Suppose for example, you found a person greeting you at the door as you entered the store. Suppose that person welcomed you to the store and asked if they could help you find anything in particular. Would that be just a little more than you have expected? Perhaps so. But that is, of course, precisely what Wal-Mart stores have done. By hiring people, often senior citizens on a part-time basis, who serve as greeters, Wal-Mart is exceeding the expectations of many discount store shoppers, and in the process, attracting a lot of customers.

But wait—that idea has been done. Are there ways we can take this a step further? Why not get someone to roam around the store wearing a special vest that says "Can I Help You Find Something?" printed on it and simply have that individual look for customers who appear to be confused or questioning a particular purchase. This individual would have to be exceptionally personable and knowledgeable about the products in the store. Wouldn't that exceed the expectations of most people in a self-service store? That's an example of an E-Plus strategy. Consistently doing little things that surprise the customer.

SIX GOLDEN E-PLUS OPPORTUNITIES: VISPAC

In my work with clients, I've refined this E-Plus idea and now see that there are at least six areas where we can use it. To help remember these we'll use the acronym, VISPAC (as in *vis*able *pac*kaging).

The six categories of E-Plus opportunities (VISPAC) are value, information, speed, personality, add-ons, and convenience. When a customer feels he or she is getting more than expected in any or all of these six areas, the likelihood of customer loyalty increases dramatically. For the next part of this chapter, we will discuss examples of VISPAC.

Apply E-Plus by creating "VISable PACkage."

Value

How can we exceed customer expectations regarding the value—the valuable-ness—of the products we sell? When people think of value, they think of some exceptional products they've owned. Perhaps it's a fifteen or twenty-year-old Kirby vacuum cleaner, a Ford pickup truck, a Western Auto freezer, or an always accurate and totally reliable tax preparation service. Maybe you have a sweater that dates back a quarter century (I do!), a set of Craftsman tools that never break, or a Timex watch that "takes a lickin' and keeps on tickin'." Each of these products may exceed

Value is a function of how long a product lasts.

one's expectations of value. Its buyer feels he got more for his money than he would have ever expected when he purchased these items.

Two Characteristics of Value. Keep in mind two characteristics of value expectations. First, customers may not fully appreciate the value of something until its long-term quality becomes evident. Conveying E-Plus value to customers may take an extended time to become evident. Second, value is always relative to the price. Indeed, a definition of value is: *the quality of a product or service relative to its price.* Some items we buy are throw-aways—inexpensive items we don't

> Value is defined as quality relative to cost. Sometimes value does not become apparent until customers become aware of the product's longevity.

expect to last. Yet even these can exceed expectations if they last a bit longer than we thought they would, or if they cost even less than we would expect.

Sometimes customers simply need to be reminded of the value they are receiving. A City Government may, for example, send information about how tax dollars are being used in the community to show its value. Some discount stores program their computers to show the list prices of products bought along side their discount prices, thus reinforcing what a good deal the customer received.

```
                BIZMART
366 E. 1300 South             Store 161
           Orem, UT 84058
SALE                61853 16104 95630
                0161 11/12/91 03:58 PM

071402303167
  REFILL,BALLPOINT              1.50
  MFG. LIST $2.50
072838120007
  MARKER RAZOR PT,              0.69
  MFG. LIST $1.29
043100171225
  FILLER PAPER PAD              1.89
  MFG. LIST $2.98
074319240334
  PAD,EASEL 27X34"              8.79
  MGF LIST $16.00
MEMBER #
PURCHASE ORDER #
               SUB TOTAL       12.87
             6.250% TAX         0.80
                  TOTAL       $13.67
                  CHECK        13.67
ACCOUNT NUMBER   00182998
AUTH 9999

               IPV LN 30380  06913047

**********  YOUR PURCHASES  **********

CATALOG LIST PRICES
WOULD HAVE COST YOU          $22.77

BIZMART'S LOW
EVERYDAY PRICES =            $12.87

******************************
YOU SAVED                     $9.90
******************************
THAT'S A SAVINGS OF             43%

   THANK YOU FOR SHOPPING AT BIZMART
```

Information

How can we exceed customer expectations by providing more, better, or clearer information that the customer can use? One of my children had knee surgery a few years ago. Following the surgery, he was assigned a physical therapist who was to teach him how to regain strength in his knees. We expected the therapist to basically tell him what exercises to do and let it go at that. But the therapist not only explained what exercises he should do but also gave him paper copies illustrating exactly how to do them, a thorough demonstration of each workout, and a follow-up phone call a few days later to see how he was doing. Little things, of course, but still an E-Plus in my mind.

Today's car salespeople no longer tell you that there is an owner's manual in the glove box you can read. Instead they often spend considerable time with customers explaining all the bells and whistles on their new car. The good ones do this even after the sale is made. This is E-Plus information giving.

A hospital client I worked with changed the signs in the hospital when it became evident that patients and guests were getting lost and installed color stripes on the corridor floors to direct people to various departments. A cellular phone dealer calls customers to see if they understand how to use all the features and offers to meet to explain them in person.

Often the best opportunities for E-Plus in information are to use different media that is customary. Computer software products are often accompanied by a learning CD or videotape program. Some advertisers like NordicTrack exercise equipment use videos both to sell and to demonstrate their products. How can your business give customers more useful information?

Another Look

Alamo E-Plusses with Information[4]

Alamo Rent-A-Car has announced that, due to continued strength of the number of international, multilingual travelers worldwide, the company now offers multilingual rental agreements printed in both English and the renter's language of choice.

Alamo North America locations, which have offered multilingual rental agreements at all U.S. locations since November 1994, maintain a record of each customer's preferred language — French, German or Spanish — along with other pertinent rental information. When the customer picks up a car, the rental contract is automatically printed in English and their language of choice, making it easier for the customer to read and understand.

Alamo North America also has multilingual capabilities at its two new Canadian locations. In Montreal, rental agreements are printed in French or, if the customer prefers, in English, Spanish, or German. In Vancouver, the rental agreement is printed in English or, if the customer prefers, in French, Spanish, or German.

Alamo Europe provides rental agreements at all its Germany locations in both German and English. In Switzerland, rental agreements in Zurich are printed in German and English, while in Geneva the rental agreements are printed in French and English. Alamo locations in all other countries print rental agreements in English.

Alamo currently serves 15 million travelers a year through 120 locations in the United States and Canada, and 85 international locations in the United Kingdom, Switzerland, Ireland, The Netherlands, Germany, Belgium, Greece, Portugal, and Austria.

Service Snapshot

Michael Krause, 16 year-old owner
of Exchange Network Services[5]

With 5,500 subscribers, Exchange Network Services is not the largest Internet service provider in the country, but I'll bet you it has the youngest boss. Sixteen-year-old Michael Krause, a high school junior, founded the company two years ago. He was running a bulletin board service out of a bedroom in his parents' home and he noticed that the chatterers had begun talking about the Internet.

"The math of the business is simple," explains Michael. "For every ten subscribers you have to buy a $200 modem. For every 300 modems, you have to buy a $3,000 terminal server." Michael persuaded his brother Daniel, a mutual fund salesman, to buy $7,000 worth of startup equipment, using his credit card to pay. The company has had positive cash flow ever since.

"We don't advertise very much," says Michael. "If you talk to your customers carefully and explain everything in language they can understand, then they tell their friends."

About 80% of Exchange Network Services' subscribers come from other costomers' referrals. "Customer service is cool," says Michael, who gets to the office every day at 2 p.m., after finishing school, and works until 6 p.m. and on Saturdays. A staff of ten people report to the young chief executive, including seven customer service representatives, four of whom work nights and weekends.

What would this little company be worth in a sale? We won't know until it's sold or goes public (my firm, by the way, may be involved in the transaction), but it's safe to say that the number should be comfortably in the seven digits. Just extrapolate from the valuations of larger Internet service providers: roughly $715 per subscriber at Net-

Com On-Line Communication Services and CompuServe, $1,000 at America Online and $2,700 at PSI Net.

What's interesting here is what it says about Internet service. The providing of access looks like just another commodity, but it isn't. If you have a knack for responding quickly to your customers' problems without spending too extravagantly on your help-line staff, you have the formula for success. Look at the turmoil in the personal computer manufacturing industry over the past decade. Anybody can make a cheap box, but not everybody can also make his customers happy.

This is a big problem for the on-line services. As their customers migrate to the Internet, how does the on-line service persuade these customers to keep them on as the access provider? The problem is not in the programming: All the on-line service must do is take its existing on-line software and tack on an Internet connection written by a handful of very skilled Unix programmers. But the marketing problem is something else. Imagine seeing an announcement when you boot up your on-line service: "Good Morning. We're going to change your subscription from our feature-rich on-line service to the more practical Internet."

Unlike AOL, NetCom doesn't have the migration job to tackle—it's already a pure Internet service provider. Under the circumstances, NetCom's low valuation is almost as big a surprise as AOL's lofty one. True, NetCom is in the red, but these connection companies are like cable TV providers in that they should be appraised more on subscriber counts than profits. (We are not engaged by NetCom.)

NetCom is adding 5,700 subscribers a week, net, and its managers keep their heads under the hood. Chief Executive David Garrison shares this with the young entrepreneur from Cleveland: He has developed customer accounting software that enables accurate per-use billing, an industry rarity. He's building a sister customer service center in Dallas. When he gets done, NetCom will have added 200 customer service experts.

"The most frequently asked question by a new subscriber is 'How do I get onto the Web?'" says Michael Krause."If they can't get the hang of it over the phone," says Michael, "I get in my car and drive out to their house."

House calls. Now that's service.

Speed

How can you exceed your customers' expectations with regard to the speed of service? Research of customer turnoffs repeatedly shows that customers dislike having to wait too long for products or services.[6] Across all types of businesses, people want timely response. My research shows that even when engaged in leisurely dining at an upscale restaurant, people still value timely service.

Federal Express and the other air freight companies claim to deliver your package by 10 o'clock the next morning, but it often arrives by 9 or 9:30. The repair office for a major office equipment company makes it a policy to tell customers precisely when the repair person can be there (thus setting an expectation) and then seeing that the service persons arrive earlier than promised (E-Plus). The reason this works so well in our culture is that people seldom arrive on time. Repair people and delivery services are often notorious for showing up late—or not at all! It's a major pet peeve of customers, yet one that can be easily fixed.

> Offering service faster than expected—even when you originally set the expectation—is a powerful form of E-Plus.

Staffing decisions affect speed. At a progressive supermarket, additional cashiers open when more than two customers are in line. Good fast-food restaurants have lunch up almost before you can order it because they staff and train extensively. Are there ways you can give customers a little faster service than they expect?

Personality

How can you exceed customer expectations with the personality of your people? Every company or organization conveys a personality to its customers. This personality is a composite of countless little behaviors exhibited by the people who work there. Friendliness, courtesy, efficiency, professionalism, and quality are all conveyed via behaviors both verbal and nonverbal.

This dimension of personality is so important that Chapter 5 will deal with it at length. For now, the question is, "How can you or your company project positive personality characteristics that exceed customer expectations?"

Often we can E-Plus our customers with our personality.

Add-Ons

How can you exceed customer expectations by giving or selling customers something else they will need or appreciate? When a shoe store clerk gives a shoehorn with a pair of new shoes or when he asks if you'd like to

> Give away something of perceived value and you tip the equity scale in your favor.

try padded inserts or a pair of lifetime guarantee socks, he is using this E-Plus approach. Sometimes add-ons are sold, sometimes given away. Both can be effective. A clerk at a supermarket hands customers a few candy kisses with the receipt, an unexpected thank you. The hotel check-in desk has a basket of complimentary apples. The paint store salesperson checks to be sure buyers have caulking and sandpaper.

The best kinds of free add-ons are those with high perceived value and low cost to the business. For example, gas stations that give away a free car wash with fill up find that such washes cost them about seven cents but have a perceived value of $2 or $3 (which is the price printed on the coupon). Free popcorn or drinks given away with video rentals cost 3 or 4 cents but have a much higher perceived value.

Obviously, this E-Plus opportunity area ties in closely with its marketing counterpart, add-on sales. Marketers have long recognized the value of trying to sell current customers something else so long as you have them here. This can backfire if it's too pushy, but most customers will not resent low-key inquiries about other products. What add-on product or service can you give your customers?

HERMAN®

**"If you buy a goldfish,
I'll throw in the aardvark."**

Add-ons can encourage customer loyalty—if they have perceived value.

Convenience

How can you exceed customer expectation by making your product or service more convenient than expected? This may be the E-Plus area with the greatest potential in today's efficiency-obsessed culture. Enhanced convenience is especially valuable in two areas: in recovery of unhappy customers and in attracting new customers.

Convenience is a great way to E-Plus customers.

The typical response to a customer with a faulty product is "bring it in and we'll replace it." But recall our example of how the Lexus handled a recall shortly after coming onto the market with their new car. Dealers called customers for an appointment to *pick up* the car and they left a loaner car for the customer. If a customer has to go through the trouble of bringing back a faulty product, you might E-Plus by offering to deliver a replacement.

Twenty years ago if you needed an oil change on your car you'd take it to a service station, leave it for the day, getting a ride to work, etc. Today we go to quick lube shops, drive in, step out of the car, have a cup of coffee in the waiting room, and ten minutes later we are back on the road. That's convenience.

> Quick-lube auto services have flourished as a response to the need for speed.

The number one restaurant food in America is pizza. But if you had to go to a pizza restaurant, order your food, and wait 20 minutes for it to be served, I doubt that it would be so popular. It's take-out and delivery services that built the pizza industry.

There remain a lot of inconveniences customers face daily. If you come up with great ideas for E-Plussing in the area of convenience, you'll have a strong competitive advantage. Shopping via the internet is one obvious approach that is just beginning to be tapped. How can you make things more convenient for your customers?

> Convenience is one of the most promising E-Plus opportunity areas because so much of what customers face today is inconvenient.

HERMAN®

"Don't bother undressing.
I'll turn up the power."

Convenience is a powerful E-Plus opportunity area.

WHERE DO GOOD E-PLUS IDEAS COME FROM?

The ideas above are, of course, simply illustrative. The possibilities for E-Plus are quite literally unlimited. E-Plus organizations constantly fish for new "little things" that can and will make huge differences. Like "Total Quality Management" (which we discuss in detail in Chapter 7), E-Plus requires constant incremental improvements. Little improvements, little innovations lead to a payoff that is enormous. E-Plus really is the master key for customer satisfaction and retention. If you're not thinking E-Plus, your competition may be.

To get a constant flow of new E-Plus ideas, ask employees at all levels of the organization to apply creativity. Work to create an environment where new ideas are tried and innocent mistakes are not punished. Have supervisors or team leaders get together regularly to brain storm new ideas. Then reward the best ideas with recognition and possibly prizes. The result of this process (which is described in more detail in Chapter 7) is a lively, vibrant, evolving organization with a strong and competitive advantage that cannot be duplicated by your competition.

Another Look

Legacy Audio

A recent Wall Street Journal article describes a small, but highly successful company that "makes stereo speakers for snobs." Legacy Audio charges as much as $12,500 for a pair of its exceptionally high-quality speakers. The company's founders, Jake Albright and Bill Dudleston, do a great job of listening to their customers and meeting their needs, as described in this excerpt:[7]

> From marketing to manufacturing to shipping, every aspect of the business was organized around the perceived customer's point of view.
>
> To build trust for Legacy's unfamiliar name, Bill designed ads showing the grandfatherly Jake in his woodworking apron—the master craftsman from central casting. When a customer called for a catalog on the toll-free line, the details of the call were added to a homegrown database. Each time a potential customer called back—audiophiles ask lots of questions—a sales agent called up details of previous conversations to the screen.
>
> As the company grew, Bill staffed the phone lines with people from the shop or the engineering lab, reckoning that hands-on experience would make the pitch more convincing. Anyone considering a purchase was invited to fax in a room layout; discussing the particulars of upholstery and floor finishes created a feeling of intimacy. Bill figured that no major competitor could ever match that level of customer interaction. "That's how you box people out of your market," he says.
>
> To make the most of the magic moment when the delivery truck arrived at a customer's home, Legacy created a fancy wooden shipping crate that prevented dings and scratches (while ending the need for environmentally incorrect plastic peanuts; such are the delicacies of selling to a high-brow crowd).
>
> And despite his love of the technical (and his degrees in math and physics), Bill insisted that every unit be tested not only electronically but by a customer's only method: listening. Over and over today, speakers are put through their paces with an extraordinary falsetto passage by the R&B artist Aaron Neville, "a complete frequency sweep," Bill says, "in four seconds."

Probes . . .

1. How does Legacy Audio apply the E-Plus concepts described in this chapter?
2. Would such attention to customers work for any kind of business?

A FINAL THOUGHT . . .

Understanding and attempting to exceed customer expectations is an ongoing challenge—and an opportunity for any business. Recognizing the power of equity theory justifies the effort needed. Progressive organizations make E-Plus idea generation an ongoing process. Expectations are moving targets, so companies can never rest on just their past actions but must progressively strive to offer better and better service as perceived by their customers.

-------------------- *Summary of Key Ideas* --------------------

⬧ E-Plus is a shorthand term for the process of exceeding customer expectations to create customer loyalty.

⬧ VISPAC is an acronym that reminds people of six areas where expectations could be exceeded. Organizations would be wise to gather employees regularly to generate ideas in each of these six areas.

⬧ Before we can exceed expectations, we must know what the customer expects now. Naive listening, focus groups, observation, and feedback techniques can help us do so.

Application Activity
E-Plus Brainstorming

Working in teams of five to ten people, imagine yourself in the role of a business you are familiar with (retail store, health care facility, insurance office, hotel/restaurant, public utility, repair shop, etc.) Using the worksheets found on pages 83 through 88, brainstorm E-Plus ideas that might be useful. Be careful to not be overly judgmental as you come up with ideas. The wilder the better in many cases. You can then go back and refine the group's best ideas.

If you decide to fish for ideas in the Personality category, read Chapter 5 before completing this assignment.

NOTES

[1] "Baby Boomers May Seek Age-Friendly Stores," in *Wall Street Journal,* July 1, 1992, p. B1. Reprinted with permission.

[2] The basic premises of equity theory can be found in Adams, J. S., "Toward an Understanding of Inequity," *Journal of Abnormal and Social Psychology,* 67 (1963): 422-36. Later studies are summarized in Berkowitz, L. and Walster, E. (Eds.) *Advances in Experimental Social Psychology,* vol. 9 (New York: Academic Press, 1976).

[3] Timm, P. "Effects of Inequity in Supervisory Communication Behaviors on Subordinates in Clerical Workgroups," unpublished doctoral dissertation, Florida State University, 1977.

[4] Transmitted via America Online. Fort Lauderdale, FL., June 9, 1995, PRNewswire.

[5] Excerpted from Silver, A.D., "Service is our most important product," *Forbes,* June 3, 1996, p. 146.

[6] DeTienne, K and Timm, P., "How Well Do Businesses Predict Customer Turnoffs? A Discrepancy Analysis," *Journal of Marketing Management* Vol. 5, No. 2, 1997.

[7] Petzinger, T. "Audio Legacy Shows Value of Feedback in Speaker Sales," *Wall Street Journal,* August 8, 1996, p. B1.

VISPAC WORKSHEET #1

VALUE. E-Plus your customers by creating a perception of value that exceeds their expectations. List ideas for clarifying or presenting an enhanced sense of value in your product or service. Consider such things as various payment options, clarity of billing so that the customer understands costs of different services, and highlighting any discounts given. Remember that value is a relationship of *quality compared to cost.* Consider such things as guarantees, packaging, etc.

After brainstorming possible ideas, put a check in the box next to ideas for further consideration.

☐

☐

☐

☐

☐

☐

☐

The best idea for implementation now is:

VISPAC WORKSHEET #2

INFORMATION. E-Plus your customers with more, better, or different information than they expect. Consider the possibility of using different media. List ideas for clarifying, improving, or presenting additional information customers may find useful as they use the product or service.

   After brainstorming possible ideas, put a check in the box next to ideas for further consideration.

☐

☐

☐

☐

☐

☐

☐

☐

The best idea for implementation now is:

VISPAC WORKSHEET #3

SPEED. E-Plus your customers by exceeding customer expectations about your efficiency or response times. List ideas for reducing delays or providing faster service than customers might anticipate. Remember that slow service is the number one complaint of customers in almost every type of business. Your task is to be faster and/or to clarify realistic expectations for customers.

After brainstorming possible ideas, put a check in the box next to ideas for further consideration.

☐

☐

☐

☐

☐

☐

☐

☐

The best idea for implementation now is:

PERSONALITY. E-Plus your customers by conveying pleasant, attentive, personable service that exceeds what they may expect. Consider any small verbal or nonverbal "message" you may be sending out. Include possible dialog ideas for telephone or personal visitors.

After brainstorming possible ideas, put a check in the box next to ideas for further consideration.

☐

☐

☐

☐

☐

☐

☐

☐

The best idea for implementation now is:

ADD-ONs. E-Plus your customers by giving or selling them something additional. List ideas for surprising them with a small gift or premium. Consider add-on products they may benefit from or need to make the best use of something they've already purchased.

After brainstorming possible ideas, put a check in the box next to ideas for further consideration.

☐

☐

☐

☐

☐

☐

☐

☐

The best idea for implementation now is:

CONVENIENCE. E-Plus your customers by making life easier for them than they expected. List ideas for enhancing their experience with your product or service. Consider such things as free delivery, in-home or in-office services, your handling follow-up details, etc.

    After brainstorming possible ideas, put a check in the box next to ideas for further consideration.

☐

☐

☐

☐

☐

☐

☐

☐

The best idea for implementation now is:

The Behaviors that Win Customer Loyalty

It's what you DO!

. . . if a man offend not in word, the same is a perfect man, and able also to bridle the whole body. Behold, we put bits in horse's mouths, that they may obey us; and we turn about their whole body.

—The Bible (James 3:2-3)

THE WAY IT IS . . .

Humorist Dave Berry tells this story:[1]

Joe [my attorney] has a client whom I'll call Charles, a mild-mannered financial officer who has never been in any kind of trouble. One evening Charles was driving home from work on the New England Thruway and came to a toll plaza. When his turn came, he pulled up to the booth and held out his $1.25. At this point, the toll-taker pulled out what Charles described as "the biggest pile of one-dollar bills I have ever seen," and started slowly counting them. A minute went by. A line of cars formed behind Charles. Another minute went by. The toll-taker kept counting. Some people behind Charles started honking. ANOTHER minute went by. Charles sat there, looking in disbelief at the toll-taker, who apparently planned to continue counting the entire pile of bills, and then, who knows, maybe read "War and Peace." In the lengthening line behind Charles, more people were honking, shouting, gesturing, possibly rummaging through their glove compartments for firearms.

Finally Charles, despite being mild-mannered, did a bad thing. In fact he did THREE bad things: (1) He made an explicit, non-toll-related suggestion to the toll-taker; (2) he threw his $1.25 into the booth; and (3) he drove away.

He did not get far, of course. Western Civilization did not get where it is today by tolerating this kind of flagrant disregard of toll procedures. Charles was swiftly apprehended by two police cars, which escorted him to the police station, where he called Joe, who managed to keep him out of prison through the shrewd legal maneuver of telling him to pay the $50 fine.

Pretty outrageous story, yes? But these kinds of things happen when employees either (1) hate their job and couldn't care less about customers, or (2) are completely ignorant of how certain behaviors come across to others. Let's give this toll-taker the benefit of the doubt and assume that he was simply unaware of how his behavior was being interpreted. That's a stretch, I know, but ignorance is pretty commonplace. Part of the toll-taker's job was undoubtedly to count the money. That may be a very important part of the job. But his timing was absurd. The implications of his actions on others were apparently not within his range of awareness.

-------------------- *Learning Objectives* --------------------

When you have studied this chapter, you should be able to

1. Recognize the role of communication in projecting behavior and describe two critical rules of communicating.

2. Name and apply 15 specific behaviors to exceed customer expectations in the area of individual personality.

3. Name seven actions that convey the organization's personality (culture) to customers.

ANYTHING CAN CONVEY A MESSAGE

Behavior is, of course, what people do. It is conveyed to others via both verbal and nonverbal communication. Our friend the toll-taker used no verbal communication (no words were spoken) but still communicated loud and clear a wide range of messages, most of which said he didn't care about his customer.

In less blatant cases, we all occasionally communicate the "wrong" message with our nonverbal behaviors. A salesperson who fails to greet a customer, a fellow worker who shows up late, a repair person who leaves a mess all communicate something. Two important rules of communication are

1. Anything can and will communicate, and
2. The receiver of the message determines what it "means."

The remainder of this chapter looks at some of the kinds of behaviors—of individuals and of organizations—that convey meaning to customers. This is by no means an exhaustive list of all possible behaviors but it does reflect some of the more common ones that associate closely with customer satisfaction.

> Any behaviors can, and often will, communicate meaning to our customers.

BEHAVIORS AND THE PERSONALITY FACTOR IN VISPAC

In Chapter 4 we discussed the role of exceeding expectations (we called it E-Plus) in creating customer loyalty. We also identified six opportunity areas for E-Plus: value, information, speed, *personality*, add-ons, and convenience. Now is the time to look more closely at personality, a powerful way to create E-Plus experiences for customers.

A customer's experience is determined by little behaviors.

Each customer encounters two interrelated personalities: the personality of the individual who serves the customer and the overall personality of the organization. This organizational personality is a reflection of the company's "culture." Culture is a composite of many factors that strengthen and reinforce individual behavior. If a company is a fun place to work, its people will convey a sense of enjoyment to customers. If the culture is more formal (say, a law firm or other professional office) this is reinforced by employee behaviors and other organizational factors which will be discussed later in this chapter.

Wal-Mart founder Sam Walton understood organizational behavior when he said, "Your people will treat your customers the way you [meaning managers] treat your people." Enthusiasm, comradeship, a sense of enjoyment, and humor quickly becomes evident to customers. Southwest Airlines, which has a culture of informality and fun at work, projects an organizational personality very different than many of its competitors. This personality has been useful both in attracting customers and attracting employees who enjoy working in such an atmosphere.

INDIVIDUAL BEHAVIORS THAT CONVEY PERSONALITY

It's the little things that mean everything. Often the subtlest behaviors can convey the most powerful messages to customers. Below are 15 important individual behaviors that, taken together, project personality. As you become aware of these, you'll quickly recognize E-Plus opportunities in each. Awareness alone can improve service yet many employees are essentially clueless to the impact of these kinds of behaviors.[2]

1. Greet Customers Like a Guest

Woody Allen once said that 80 percent of success is just showing up. In customer service, 80 percent of success is just treating the customer like a guest who just showed up. When guests come to your home, you greet them, right? You say "hello," or "hi there." Yet we've all had the experience of being totally ignored by service people in some businesses. A friendly greeting is one of those little things that mean a lot.

Greet your customer promptly. Studies have clocked the number of seconds people had to wait to be greeted in several businesses. Researchers then asked customers how long they'd been waiting. In every case, the customer's estimate of the time elapsed was much longer than the actual time. A customer waiting 30 or

> The failure to be greeted creates stress in a customer.

40 seconds often feels like it's been three or four minutes! Time drags when you're being ignored.

A prompt greeting reduces customer stress. Why would customers feel stress? Remember, they are usually on unfamiliar turf. They are likely to feel somewhat uncomfortable. You work there every day; they are just visiting. A prompt, friendly greeting starts to relax the customer and greases the wheels of smooth service.

Speak up. Verbally greet a customer within 10 seconds of the time he or she comes into your store or approaches your work location. Even if you are busy with another customer or on the phone, pause to say hello and let them know that you'll be ready to help them soon.

Get the customer committed. Did you ever wonder why some fast food restaurants send a clerk out to write your order on a sheet of paper while you are waiting in line? Think about it. You tell the person what you want and she marks it on a slip of paper which she then gives back to you to present at the cash register where the order is called out. Why is this done? It is simply a way of getting the customer committed. If no one greeted you or wrote your order you may be more likely to leave before ordering. Psychologically, you feel like you've "ordered" so you stay in line and follow through with your lunch purchase.

So, greet each customer promptly, verbally if possible, and try to commit them as soon as they come into your business or work area.

2. Break the Ice

The best way to start a conversation depends on what the customer needs. In many cases, especially in retail stores, customers first need to be reassured that this is a "nice friendly place" to do business. They need to dispel worries about being high-pressured into buying. To do so, use a non-threatening ice breaker. Often customers want to browse; get the feel of the place before they commit to doing business.

The best ice breaker for the browser can be an off-topic, friendly comment. Some good ones might be:

- A *compliment* ("That's a very sharp tie you're wearing." or "Your children are sure cute. How old are they?")
- *Weather-related or local interest comments* ("Isn't this sunshine just beautiful?" or "Some snowfall, isn't it?" or "How about those Bulls last night?")
- *"Small talk"* Look for cues about one's interests in sports, jobs, mutual acquaintances, past experiences, etc. Then initiate a relevant comment.

If your browser seems to be focusing attention on a product (say he is holding several shirts or is looking at a particular line of products), he can be reclassified as a "focused shopper." *The best ice breaker for the focused shopper* is one that is more specific to the buying decision. It may:

- *anticipate the customer's questions* ("What size are you looking for, sir?" or "Can I help you select a _____?")
- *provide additional information* ("Those shirts are all 25 percent off today" or "We have additional _____ in the stock room.")
- *offer a suggestion or recommendation* ("Those striped suits are really popular this season" or "If you need help with measurements our estimators can figure out what you'll need.")

Be attentive to the customer's needs. Give them time to browse if that's what they need, but be responsive to them in helping make a buying decision when they are ready to buy.

> Learn what "ice-breaker" lines work best for different kinds of customers.

In non-retailing organizations, use friendly, sincere expression of willingness to serve. Asking how you can help works well.

3. Compliment Freely and Sincerely

It only takes a second to say something nice to a person and it can add enormous goodwill. Say something complimentary to your internal and external customers. Safe ground for sincere compliments may focus on:

- *Some article of clothing they are wearing* ("I like that tie!" or "That's a beautiful sweater you have on.")
- *Their children* ("Your little boy is really cute" or "How old is your daughter. She's beautiful.")
- *Their behavior* ("Thanks for waiting. You've been very patient" or "I noticed you checking the _____. You're a careful shopper.")
- *Something they own* ("I like your car. What year is it?" or "I noticed your championship ring. Did you play on that team?")

To get yourself in the habit of complimenting, try this: Set a goal to give 10 sincere compliments each day. Make it a habit and you'll see a sharp increase in your personal popularity. People love to be complimented. And, of course, complimenting internal customers (e.g., co-workers) can help create a supportive and pleasant work climate.

> Many people are too hesitant to give compliments. People love to receive a sincere compliment. Make it a habit to do so.

4. Call People by Name

A person's name is his or her favorite sound. We appreciate it when people make the effort to find out and use our name in addressing us. When appropriate, introduce yourself to the customer and ask his or her name. If this isn't appropriate, such as when you are waiting on a line of customers, you can often get the customer's name from their check, credit card, order form, or other paperwork.

But don't be overly familiar too quickly. You are normally safe calling people Mr. Smith or Ms. Jones but may be seen as rude if you call them

> Use your customer's name if given the opportunity. It builds the relationship.

Homer and Marge. (This is especially true when younger employees are dealing with older customers.) Better to err on the side of being too formal. If people prefer first-name address, they'll tell you so.

5. Talk to Customers with Your Eyes

Even in situations where you may not be able to say hello out loud, or give undivided attention to a customer right away, you can make eye contact. Simply looking at your customer tells them much about your willingness to serve. Eye contact creates a bond between you and the customer. It conveys your interest in communicating further. Here is a personal example where the wrong message was conveyed:

> I once went into a very small watch repair shop. The shop was no more than ten feet square. I'd heard that the proprietor was a real expert at repairing timepieces and his prices were good. As I squeezed into his tiny shop he was serving another customer. I stood not more than five feet away from him for about five minutes before he acknowledged me. It got pretty uncomfortable. Once he finished with the customer ahead of me he was attentive and effective, but he ran a real risk of losing me before he got a chance to show me what he could do—simply because it was uncomfortable standing there without being acknowledged. All he would have needed to do was say hello and let me know that he would be with me momentarily.

> Establishing eye contact can convey a message that you are willing to serve them.

As with your greeting, the timing is important. The 10-second rule also applies here. Make eye contact with a customer within 10 seconds, even if you are busy with another person. As with the spoken greeting, you don't have to interrupt what you are doing with another customer. Just a pause and a quick look captures new customers into an obligation to deal with you further, greatly reducing the chance they'll feel ignored and leave.

When working with customers, be sensitive to *how* you look at them. Communication expert Bert Decker[3] says that the three "Is" of eye communication are intimacy, intimidation and involvement. Intimacy (like when we're expressing love) and intimidation (when we want to exert power) are both communicated by looking at another person for a long period—from 10 seconds to a minute or more.

Making happy customers begins with simple eye contact.

But most communication in business settings calls for Decker's third "I"—involvement. In our culture, people create involvement by looking at the other person for 5- to 10-second periods before looking away briefly. This is generally comfortable for people. If you look away more often than that, you may be seen as "shifty" or suspicious; if you lock in eye contact for longer, it feels like intimidation or intimacy.

> Eye contact, or lack of it, conveys powerful messages to customers.

6. Ask Often: "How'm I Doing?"

Legendary politician and former New York City mayor Ed Koch would constantly ask his constituents, "How'm I doing?" The phrase became his tag line. There is some evidence that he even listened to their answers. After all he survived as mayor of the Big Apple for many years. We can learn something from the Koch question.

Businesses need to ask that question in as many ways as possible. In addition to more formalized measurement and feedback systems, employees need to demonstrate an attitude of receptiveness. Being receptive to the comments and criticisms of people is challenging and, at times, frustrating. It takes a lot of courage not only to accept criticism but to actually request it! Nevertheless, some of your best ideas come from the correction others give you.

> An attitude of receptiveness is revealed by a willingness to ask questions—and listen to the answers.

7. Listen with More than Your Ears

Since so few people are really good listeners, this skill provides an excellent *E-Plus* opportunity. There is no such thing as an unpopular listener. Almost everyone becomes more interesting when he stops talking and starts listening. Pay attention to your talk-listen ratio. Are you giving the customer at least equal time?

To be a better listener, use these ideas:

- *Judge the content* of what people are saying, *not the way they are saying it*. Customers may not have the "right" words, but they know what they need better than anyone else.
- *Hold your fire*. Don't jump to make judgments before your customer has finished talking.
- *Work at listening*. Maintain eye contact and discipline yourself to listen to what is being said. Tune out those thoughts that get you thinking about something else.
- *Resist distractions*. Make the customer the center of your attention.
- *Seek clarification* from customers so you fully understand their needs. Do this in a non-threatening way using sincere, open-ended questions.

8. Say Please and Thank You

At the risk of sounding like one of those books about "things I learned in kindergarten," *be polite*. It may seem old-fashioned and some customers may not be as polite to you, but that's not *their* job. In a recent "Dear Abby" column the writer complained about sales people who said "there you go" to conclude a transaction. That kind of comment is not an appropriate substitute for thanking the customer.

Please and *Thank you* are powerful words for building customer rapport and creating customer loyalty. They are easy to say and well worth the effort.

9. Reassure the Customer's Decision to Do Business with You

Buyer's remorse can set in pretty fast, especially when people make a large purchase. At the time of sale, you can inoculate against remorse by reassuring the customer that they've made a good purchasing decision.

Phrases like, "I'm sure you'll get many hours of enjoyment out of this," or "Your family will love it" can help reassure and strengthen the buyer's resolve to follow through with the purchase and, as importantly, feel good about it.

A government agency might say, "I'll bet you're glad that's over with for another year," or "I'll handle the renewal—you've done all that is necessary."

A powerful tool for reassuring is the telephone. One consulting approach for bank executives shows how important customer calls can be. As part of a training session, the executives develop a simple script and immediately go to the phones to call some of their customers. The conversation goes something like this:

> "Hello, I'm Chris Wilson from Major Bank. I just wanted to call to let you know that we appreciate your business and would be interested in any suggestions you might have for additional ways we could serve you."

That's about it. Then they let the customer talk. The results: Customers are astounded that their banker would actually call and that he or she wasn't trying to sell anything! The image of the bank's service goes up sharply.

10. Smile

As the old adage goes, "Smile. It'll make people wonder what you've been up to." But more importantly, it'll tell customers that they came to the right place and are on friendly grounds.

Keep in mind that a smile originates in two places, the mouth and the eyes. A lips-only version looks pasted on, insincere. It's like saying "cheese" when being photographed. It doesn't fool anyone. In fact it might scare them away!

> A genuine smile originates in the eyes, not the mouth.

The eyes, however, are the windows to the soul and tell the truth about your feelings toward people. So smile with your eyes and your mouth. Let your face show that you're glad your guest arrived. Remember, you are not dressed for work until you put on a smile.

Some people smile more readily than others.
July 19, 1994, The Wall Street Journal—Permission,
Cartoon Features Syndicate

Now, in fairness, some people smile more readily than others. For some a more serious facial expression is comfortable and natural. But in American culture, a smile is both expected and appreciated when one is meeting people. If you don't smile spontaneously, practice it. It need not be a Cheshire Cat, ear-to-ear grin (in fact that may *really* get people wondering about you) but just a pleasant, natural smile. Look too at your eyebrows. Some people knit their brows and appear to be scowling, even when they don't intend to. Look at yourself in the mirror. Work on facial expression as an actor might.

11. Use Good Telephone Techniques

Telephone use calls for some special behaviors, especially if your only contact with customers is via the phone. A key to successful phone use is to simply *remember that your customer cannot see you.* Your challenge is to make up for all that lost nonverbal communication by using your voice effectively. Chapter 8 goes into depth about telephone techniques, but for now, let's review a few key behaviors:

> Remember that your telephone customer can't see you and adjust your behaviors accordingly.

- *Give the caller your name.* Let the caller know who you are just as you would in a face-to-face situation (via a name tag or desk plaque).
- *Smile into the phone.* Somehow people can hear a smile over the phone! Some telephone pros place a mirror in front of them while they're on the phone to remind them that facial expression can transmit through the wires..
- *Keep your caller informed.* If you need to look up information, tell the customer what you are doing. Don't leave them holding a dead phone with no clue as to whether you are still with them.
- *Invite the caller to get to the point.* Use questions such as "How can I assist you today?" or "What can I do for you?"
- *Commit to requests of the caller.* Tell the caller specifically what you will do and when you will get back to them. ("I'll check on this billing problem and get back to you by five this afternoon, okay?")
- *Thank the caller.* This lets the caller know when the conversation is over.
- *Let your voice fluctuate in tone, rate, and loudness.* You hold people's attention by putting a little life into your voice. Express honest reactions in expressive ways. Let your voice tones be natural and friendly.
- *Use hold carefully.* People hate being put on hold. When it's necessary, explain why and break in periodically to let them know they haven't been forgotten. If what you're doing will take longer than a

few minutes, ask the caller if you can call them back. *Write down your commitment to call back and don't miss it.*

- *Use friendly, tactful words.* Never accuse the customer of anything; never convey that their request is an imposition.[4]

12. Watch Your Timing

Nothing impresses so significantly as immediate follow-through. Successful sales people follow up with customers (usually by phone) to see that their purchases are satisfactory. Some sales people do this occasionally when they have a little spare time; the more successful do it regularly at scheduled times. Likewise, the best customer-oriented people outside of sales make commitments to customers and *always follow up*.

A simple form can help you follow up with customers and avoid commitments from dropping through the cracks. Make up your form in a notebook or on separate sheets. Include four columns as shown on page 101.

13. Reach Out and Touch Them

Physical touch is a powerful form of communication. Take an opportunity to shake hands with a customer or even pat him on the back, if appropriate.

A study of bank tellers shows the power of touch. Tellers were taught to place change in the hand of the customer rather than place it on the counter. Researchers found that customer perceptions of the bank rose sharply among customers who had been touched. In a similar study, servers who touched their restaurant customers when serving the food or giving change or a receipt found their tips increased dramatically.

Among internal customers and co-workers, a literal pat on the back can build instant rapport. But don't over-do it, some people resent others who seem too "touchy-feelie." Recognize different preferences; try touching behavior but be willing to adjust if the person seems uncomfortable or ill at ease. And, of course, the key word here is appropriateness. Never touch a person in a manner that could be interpreted as overly intimate or having sexual overtones.

> Appropriate touching is a powerful form of communication. But be sure it is socially and personally acceptable.

14. Enjoy People and Their Diversity

J. D. Salinger said, "I am a kind of paranoid in reverse. I suspect people of plotting to make me happy." With an attitude like that we'd look forward to every meeting with every customer. Of course, we quickly learn

CUSTOMER FOLLOW-UP FORM

Date	Commitment made (name, phone no., what promised)	When Due	Done

that some customers do not seem to be plotting to make us happy. Most are very pleasant. Some are unusual. A few are downright difficult.

| Try to keep your mind void of excessive criticism or cynicism. |

Every person is different; each has a unique personality. But the kind of people who tend to bug us the most are the ones who are *not like us*. Accept this diversity and learn to enjoy it. Know that peoples' needs are basically the same at some level and that treating them as guests will create the most goodwill, most of the time.

Work on verbal discipline: Confine your "self-talk"—those internal conversations in your mind— and your comments to others to focus on the positive and avoid being judgmental. Instead of saying, "Can you believe that ugly dress on that lady?" avoid comment or say, in a nonjudgmental way, "She dresses interestingly." Instead of saying, "This guy will nickel and dime me to death," say "This customer is very cost-conscious."

At times you'll have to force yourself to avoid the negative and judgmental—but you can accept the challenge and make a game out of it. Sincerely try for one full day to *avoid saying anything negative or judgmental* about another person. If you make it through the day, shoot for another day. Verbal discipline can become a habit that pays off. You'll find yourself enjoying people more.

15. Maintain a Positive Attitude about Selling

Many people hold some imagined negative stereotype about selling. Customer-contact people sometimes refuse to call themselves salespeople, preferring terms like associate or even consultant. Yet everyone is in sales to some degree. We constantly sell (convince, persuade, whatever term you prefer) other people on ourselves, our products or services, and our company.

| Everyone is in sales, regardless of job title. |

Like any profession, selling requires professional skills and attitudes. But often these skills and attitudes are different than one might think. For example, it surprises some people to find that you do not need to be an extrovert to be successful at selling. Quiet, thoughtful people often are very successful. A quiet self-confidence is more important than "techniques." Elwood Chapman, who has trained thousands of sales people, says that you will likely be good at sales if you agree with statements like these:[5]

- I can convert strangers into friends quickly and easily.
- I can attract and hold the attention of others even when I have not met them.

- I love new situations.
- I'm intrigued with the psychology of meeting and building a good relationship with someone I do not know.
- I would enjoy making a sales presentation to a group of executives.
- When dressed for the occasion, I have great confidence in myself.
- I do not mind using the telephone to make appointments with people I don't know.
- I enjoy solving problems.
- Most of the time, I feel secure.

There is certainly nothing demeaning about selling a product or service.

Self-Analysis

How Do You Measure Up?

Below is a list of the 15 individual behaviors we've discussed thus far in this chapter. Be completely honest in evaluating how well you do with each. There is nothing wrong with admitting shortcomings, indeed it is far more damaging to deny them. After rating yourself on the scale, go back through the list and circle the plus (+) or minus (-) to indicated how you *feel* about your response. If you are comfortable with your answer, circle the (+). If you wish you could honestly answer otherwise, circle the (-).

The scale meanings: N = never; O = occasionally; S = sometimes; M = most of the time; A = always.

	N	O	S	M	A	+	−	Goal:
1. I greet all customers like guests.	N	O	S	M	A	+	−	
2. I use appropriate ice breakers.	N	O	S	M	A	+	−	
3. I compliment people freely and often..	N	O	S	M	A	+	−	
4. I call customers by their name..	N	O	S	M	A	+	−	
5. I make and maintain eye contact with customers.	N	O	S	M	A	+	−	
6. I often ask for feedback to find out how I'm doing..	N	O	S	M	A	+	−	
7. I listen well.	N	O	S	M	A	+	−	
8. I always say *please* and *thank you*.	N	O	S	M	A	+	−	

9. I reassure customer's
   decisions to do business
   with me.   N   O   S   M   A   +   −
10. I smile freely and often.   N   O   S   M   A   +   −
11. I know and use good
    telephone techniques.   N   O   S   M   A   +   −
12. I am always sensitive to
    timing and follow up with
    customers.   N   O   S   M   A   +   −
13. I appropriately touch
    customers when possible.   N   O   S   M   A   +   −
14. I enjoy people and their
    diversity.   N   O   S   M   A   +   −
15. I have good attitudes about
    "selling" to customers.   N   O   S   M   A   +   −

For each item where you circled a minus sign, write a goal for improvement. Make this goal specific and measurable if possible.

ORGANIZATIONAL BEHAVIORS THAT CONVEY THE CULTURE

In addition to the individual behaviors described above, a customer also assesses the personality of the entire organization by looking at group behaviors and attitudes. The communication rule that anything can and will communicate still applies for these behaviors, of course. The composite result of group and individual behaviors convey much about the culture of the organization. If the customer likes your culture, you are well on your way to building satisfaction and loyalty. Here are some organizational behaviors to consider.

1. The Company's Appearance and Grooming

From the moment we meet people, we begin to size them up. We begin to draw conclusions about them almost immediately. What we decide about their trustworthiness and ability is largely a factor of *first impressions,* and, as the old saying goes, you only get one chance to make that first impression.

The appearance of an organization's employees is one of the first things seen by customers. Dress standards can set a company apart from the competition and create an E-Plus experience. One way this can be done is by looking at what other *successful* companies are doing. You need not be a copycat or wear an outfit you hate, but do consider what other role models do. And then meet or exceed their appearance.

An owner of an auto repair shop tried an experiment. Each of his repair people was paid on commission for the amount of repair work they brought in. He invited the mechanics to volunteer to change their dress and grooming. Several agreed to cut their hair shorter, shave daily, and wear clean uniforms. The outcome was a good example of E-plus: Those who improved their appearance generated far more repeat business than the others. The customers would ask for the better dressed mechanics, and those who chose to dress and groom themselves in the "old way" found themselves getting less work.

> Employee appearance can have a dramatic effect on business success, especially if it exceeds the expectations of the customers.

Remember, of course, that the key word in dress and grooming is *appropriate*. Sales people in a surf shop would look foolish in three-piece suits; an undertaker would look ludicrous in a Hawaiian sport shirt. To overcome problems of individual differences that may be inappropriate, some organizations issue uniforms. These may be coveralls, full uniforms, or partial uniforms such as blazers, vests, or work shirts. Some employees welcome these (they save on the costs of a wardrobe) while some resist the sameness of the uniformed look.

Determine what level of professionalism you want to convey to your customers, then create a look that projects your competence. Your customers notice these things.

2. Check the Appearance of Your Work Area

"A cluttered desk is the sign of a cluttered mind," says the desk plaque. Likewise a cluttered work area conveys a sense of disorganization and low professionalism. Look around you and see what your customer sees. Is merchandise displayed attractively? Is the place clean and tidy? Does the work space look like an organized, efficient place?

Check, too, for barriers. Often people arrange their work space with a desk, counter, or table between them and the customer. While sometimes this is necessary, often it creates a barrier—both physical and psychological—between the customer and the one serving. Try inviting customers to sit beside your desk with you instead of across from you. Try using a small round table, especially when customers need to read materials you give them. Some auto dealerships have removed all sales-

> Round tables rather than imposing desks can convey a sense of cooperation rather than opposition between customers and sales people.

office desks and replaced them with small round tables. Now the customer and sales person sit around the table and work together to make a deal. You don't feel like you are on opposite sides, in "combat" with each other, when the table is round.

Finally, look for customer comfort. Are your customers invited to sit in a comfortable chair? Does your office or store invite them to relax? Are waiting areas furnished with reading materials, perhaps a TV? Are vending machines available? Is the vending area kept clean?

A small auto body shop I visited surprised me. It had a waiting room that looked like a living room in a nice home. Easy chairs, a TV, coffee table with recent magazines, even fresh flowers.

Some organizations are less than friendly.
By permission of Johnny Hart and Creators Syndicate, Inc.

Recently, auto makers have begun to emphasize ways to make their car lots and showrooms, many of which are decades old, more attractive and customer friendly. Some now feature landscaped settings with benches and pathways, different display areas for each auto brand, and interactive systems with screens that show how elements like paint colors and upholstery look together. Take a look at your work areas from the customer's viewpoint.[6]

Service Snapshot

Banks Hang Up on Pesky Customers

What's wrong with this picture?[7] Some loud and clear messages are communicated to customers by these banks.

> As if it weren't bad enough that banks are charging extra fees to serve you at an ATM or even the teller's window, now you may have to pay a fee to call your bank or credit card issuer's customer service telephone line. Or if you phone repeatedly—even to check your balance—

you may get an unfriendly letter that scolds you for calling the bank too often.

Some of the biggest financial institutions in the country, including Bank of America and Wells Fargo, are levying punitive fees on frequent callers. Others, including Capital One and Navy Federal Credit Union, are considering similar charges. "Banks have never been famous for customer service, and now some are using customer service departments to generate fees," says Larry Cohn, a senior vice-president at PaineWebber.

In the past year Wells Fargo limited customers to three free calls a month; Bank of America imposed a six-call limit. After that, callers are automatically charged 50 cents for each call to an automated information system and $1.50 if they speak to a customer representative.

Capital One isn't charging fees—yet. But it sent letters to about 50,000 customers the bank identified as excessive callers urging them to stop phoning the customer service department so often. The letter reads: "While an occasional inquiry is to be expected, we ask that in the future you limit your phone calls to only those which are truly necessary."

The bank claims that a large number of customers called more than 100 times in a year, and that one person called 700 times. But some customers who received the letter say they called only once or twice—or had to call several times to resolve a single problem. It seems Capital One "cast its net too wide," says Ruth Susswein, executive director of Bankcard Holders of America. Capital One spokeswoman Diana Sun says the bank didn't mean to offend anyone. "We assumed someone who got the letter and had called because of a problem wouldn't think it applied to them," she says. Some of the "problem customers" are taking their business elsewhere.

3. Correspond Regularly

An athletic shoe store and a rental car agency are good examples of this simple idea. A week after purchasing some running shoes, customers receive a handwritten note from the store owner simply thanking them for buying. No fancy prose, it expresses appreciation for their business and invites them to return. A one or two sentence message. An airport car rental agency has employees write thank you notes to customers when the desk is not busy. The notes are hand written on the company letterhead and personalized to mention the type of car rented. They thank the customer and invite them to rent again the next time they are in town. The cost of doing this is practically nil since the desk is busy when flights are coming in but then has slow periods in between. Why have employees waste time when it's slow?

Don't let your customer forget you. Another way to not let customers forget you is to send them information about upcoming sales, changes in policies, new promotions, etc.. Keep the customer tied in. Likewise, discount coupons or special hours for preferred customers are often appreciated.

> Maintain an open channel of communication with customers via mailings.

A print shop sends all customers a monthly package of coupons, flyers, and samples including a printed motivational quote on parchment paper suitable for framing. Additional copies of the quote are available free for the asking. The mailing acts as a reminder of the quality of work the shop can do as well as a promotion.

4. Get the Customer Doing Something

Telling people about your products or services isn't usually enough. Showing them how it works is much better. But to really serve your customers, get them involved and exposed to your corporate culture—get their hands on your products in some way and they'll feel better about you and your company.

Studies of the most successful computer sales people, for example, show that they encourage customers to sit down at the computer as soon as possible to get them playing with it. They don't dazzle (or confuse) the customer with hi-tech jargon or even information about the machine's capabilities. They get them *doing something*. Likewise, the best auto sales people invite customers to sit in or test drive the car right away.

Other, less obvious ways to get people doing something:

- Personally hand them a shopping cart or basket
- Ask them to begin filling out paperwork
- Get them to touch or sample the product
- Offer a piece of candy or a fruit, while they wait
- Offer a product flyer, information packet, video presentation, or sample to review.

> Get customers doing something with you to expose them to your culture.

It doesn't matter so much *what* they do, so long as they begin to do something.

5. Use Hoopla and Fun

People enjoy working in an organization where they have fun. Successful companies have regular rituals, whether it be Friday afternoon popcorn, birthday parties, or employee of the month celebrations, that everyone gets involved in. Excellent organizations are fun places to work, they create rituals of their own.

As a manager at a utility company, I initiated frequent sales contests, complete with skits and prizes. Each time a particular product was sold, the service representative could pop a balloon and find inside of that balloon a prize ranging from a $10 bill to a coupon good for a piece of pie in the company cafeteria. Employees loved it and got involved.

Other ideas:

- Employee (or hero) of the week/month recognition
- Awards luncheons (include some tongue-in-cheek "awards")
- Win a day off with pay
- Casual dress days
- Halloween costume day
- Family picnics

Don't fall into the trap of thinking these things are hokey. Employees at all levels enjoy celebrations and hoopla and their effects spread to the customer.

6. Reward the Right Actions

Fairly often, organizations inadvertently reward one behavior while hoping for something else. In all too many cases an organization *hopes* something will happen but actually rewards an opposite behavior. For example: A company rewards individuals and departments for never receiving complaints. The hope is that receiving no complaints means we are doing a good job. The reality, however, may well be that no complaints are heard because the complaints are simply being suppressed. Customers have no effective way to voice a complaint. Instead, they just quit doing business with the company.

As we discussed earlier, it's not bad news to receive a complaint, it *is* bad news to suppress a complaint. Some percentage of customers will always be less than satisfied, and ignoring them does no good. Quite the contrary. It makes sense to draw out those customer concerns so that they can be addressed and corrected. As someone once said, "Even the ostrich leaves one end exposed."

> Companies sometimes reward "A" while hoping for "B."

Here are some other examples of possible reward conflicts where the wrong behaviors may be rewarded and the right behaviors ignored:

- Rewarding employees for fast transaction handling when the customer may be left uninformed or may resent being rushed along.

Example: The restaurant that encourages employees to get the customer fed and out may create unhappy customers who prefer to eat more slowly. Or: A sale is completed quickly but the electronic equipment buyer does not understand how to work the features of his VCR before he leaves the dealership.

- Encouraging salespeople to "cooperate with each other to best meet the customer needs" while paying a straight commission. Example: Salespeople practically trip over each other to approach the new customer before the other guy gets him.
- Encouraging employees to send thank-you notes to customers but never allowing on-the-job time to do so. This creates the impression that it really isn't that important.
- Constantly stressing the need to reduce the amount of return merchandise by docking the pay of clerks who accept too many returns. Result: Customers encounter reluctance to take back unsatisfactory products.
- Paying people by the hour instead of by the task accomplished. Hourly wages are simpler to administer but they basically pay people for using up time!

Check your organization. Are you really rewarding the right behaviors?

The reward system within an organization needs to be tilted to the advantage of the employee who provides excellent service. Any rewards should be given in direct relationship to the employee's contribution to customer service consistent with the theme you've selected.

Rewards take many forms, some obvious, some more subtle:

- Salary and cash bonuses
- Prizes and awards
- Promotions and job enrichment
- Preferred work locations, better offices, larger desks
- Work scheduling flexibility
- Pins, badges, uniforms
- Reserved parking space
- "Employee of the week (or month)" recognition
- Compliments, spoken or in writing
- Surprise recognition parties or celebrations
- Lunches or banquets
- Newsletter writeups

Management is only limited by it's imagination when it comes to rewarding employees. But the most important point is that *managers reward the right actions and results.*

7. Stay Close after the Sale

Customers hate a love-'em-and-leave-'em relationship. Yet many companies offer just that. Once the sale is made the customer goes back to feeling like a stranger. *Look for opportunities to contact the customer after the sale.* Establish an ongoing friendship and they'll keep coming back.

Some ideas for contacting the customer after the sale:

- Mail thank-you notes
- Call to be sure the product/service met their needs
- Send out new-product information
- Send clippings of interest or newsworthy information that may reassure the customer of his good purchasing decision
- Send birthday and holiday cards
- Invite them to participate in a focus group
- Call to thank them for referrals.

Another Look

Sour Smell of Poor Customer Service[8]

The drive to "listen to the customer" is the new mantra for American business, and customer service is the latest growth industry for consultants. Boardrooms are reverberating with the sound of CEOs preaching the gospel of "getting close to our customers." However, there is a remarkable chasm between these head-office professions of commitment to the customer and the actual behavior toward those self-same customers down the line.

This fall, in the course of conducting 22 marketing workshops across the U.S., our firm found that gap to be painfully evident.

We used a variety of hotels for these workshops, including three from a chain that has become synonymous with customer service (I'll refrain from naming this chain because I have consulted with one of its chief competitors).

We were asked by all three to fill out slightly different credit applications. The credit department in each case insisted that a copy of its sister hotel's form was insufficient and that only its own would do; only under duress did it accept a copy of the credit application from another member of the chain (which, incidentally, contained all the information it asked for, simply in a different format).

In arranging for people to register attendees at these workshops, we dealt with one of the national chains of temporary staff, Office Overload. We were pleased to find that we could deal with one individual who would arrange all the bookings for us. But billing was another matter. No matter how hard we tried, we could not get consolidated billing. As a result, we received 22 bills from 22 different locations—and had to write 22 checks for $200 or less.

Out for dinner with a client after one of the workshops, we walked into the local outpost of a well-known chain of midpriced Italian restaurants, Olive Garden. At our request for a nonsmoking table, we got the response that every abstainer will recognize: "It will take about 20 minutes for a table in nonsmoking, but there's a table right at the edge of the smoking section that I can let you have right away."

I countered with what seemed to me a perfectly reasonable proposition. "Seat us in smoking for now and move us into nonsmoking when that opens up."

The reply, "I'm sorry, sir, I can't do that," provoked an unsympathetic response. "Do you mean to tell me that with modern technology we can send a man to the moon and bring him back, but you can't start us at one table and then move us to another?"

We did ultimately get our way—but only grudgingly and with the clear sense that we were being unreasonable in the extreme.

This is by no means an exhaustive list. Any traveler can regale you with tales of unresponsive, uncaring service. Which leads to the simple question: What's going on here? How is it that these paragons of customer commitment at the head office ignore, insult and otherwise frustrate customers in their actual dealings?

The sources of this problem are more numerous than can be dealt with here—ranging from front-line employees and middle management entrenched in old, familiar patterns to a simple failure to communicate on the part of senior management.

There is, however, another factor at work here—what, for lack of a better description, I call the "Takla syndrome." Early in my career, business took me to a pulp and paper mill in Takla, a small community in the interior of British Columbia.

As we approached, I was hit by a distinct and overwhelming odor, which I subsequently discovered was sulfur. As discreetly as I could, I asked my client, a longtime resident, how people put up with the smell. His response: "Smell? What smell?"

He was quite serious. After awhile, people who lived in Takla simply became inured to the smell—they didn't notice it anymore. In fact, for them, it didn't exist.

And that, I believe, is what's happening when we encounter those nonresponsive employees. Often, they've lived with the smell of poor customer service for so long that they don't notice it anymore.

If you want to effect change, the first thing you have to do is get your people to understand the frustrations your customers face, to get them to walk through the buying experience from the customer's point of view.

There are many methods that will help sensitize front-line staff. One of the simplest and most effective is to videotape some customers actually talking about what they find frustrating in dealing with your company. It's remarkable how quickly you see lights go on when those tapes get played back.

How you sensitize your employees doesn't really matter. What is important is that you understand the barrier represented by the Takla syndrome. Unless you deal with this problem, all your talk about listening to the customer will just frustrate those of your clients foolish enough to believe that you actually mean it.

Mr. Richards is president of a Toronto-based marketing consultancy and a frequent speaker on customer service.

Probes

1. What are some of the specific behaviors cited in this reading that caused the customer's dissatisfaction?
2. To what extent do the customer turnoffs arise from value, systems, and people?
3. What actions would you, as a manager, take to remedy the customer problems described in this article?

A FINAL THOUGHT

Individual and organizational behaviors are conveyed to customers via little things. Often people are unaware of how they are coming across and, as such, are at a distinct disadvantage. Broadening our awareness of how other people read our verbal and nonverbal messages is a useful step in improving customer service.

Likewise, just as individuals project their behaviors to customers, so do organizations. The company's collective behavior patterns constitute its culture and may be perceived as favorable or unfavorable by customers (internal and external). The ways managers and leaders interact with subordinates and associates will have considerable impact on the way all people behave toward customers.

-------------------- *Summary of Key Ideas* --------------------

▶ Behavior is what people do. It is conveyed via verbal or nonverbal communication.

▶ Individual actions as well as organizational behaviors convey messages to customers which may be productive or counterproductive to their perception of service received.

▶ Any behaviors (or lack of behaviors) can communicate; the receiver of the message (e.g., the customer) determines what the message means.

▶ Exceeding expectations in the area of personality (as discussed in our VISPAC acronym in Chapter 4) depends on both individual actions and the organization's behaviors or culture.

◗ Individual behaviors that impact customer service include greeting customers, breaking the ice by initiating conversation, complimenting, calling people by name, establishing and maintaining eye contact, asking for feedback, listening skillfully, reassuring customer buying decisions, smiling, using good telephone techniques, being sensitive to timing, appropriate touching behaviors, enjoying people, and being positive about selling.

◗ Organizational behaviors that tell the customer about your culture include the appearance and grooming of employees, the appearance of work areas, the frequency and quality of correspondence with customers, the propensity to get customers doing something relevant to the buying decision, use of hoopla and fun to celebrate company successes, reward systems that motivate appropriate employee behaviors, and staying close to the customer after the sale.

Application Activity
Does Behavior Influence Customer Loyalty?

This chapter implies a strong relationship between behaviors (of individuals and organizations) and the likelihood of customer loyalty. Let's test that idea.

Below are two simple data-gathering forms. The first lists the behaviors discussed in the chapter and invites customers to rate these. The second form asks three simple questions about customer loyalty. We call this the Customer Loyalty Index (CLI).

Your task is to gather input by interviewing ten or more customers of a business or organization. Use the same business for all responses. Follow the interview guide word-for-word. Have each respondent answer "yes," "no," or "unsure/not-applicable."

Interview Guide

Part I. Behavior Questionnaire

When you last did business with _____ did the employees there

1. greet you promptly?	Yes	No	? or NA
2. use opening comments to help you feel at ease?	Yes	No	? or NA
3. compliment you in any way?	Yes	No	? or NA
4. call you by your name?	Yes	No	? or NA

5. make and maintain eye contact
   with you?   Yes   No   ? or NA
6. ask for feedback from you in any
   way?   Yes   No   ? or NA
7. listen carefully to your needs or
   wants?   Yes   No   ? or NA
8. say please and thank you?   Yes   No   ? or NA
9. reassure your decisions to do business
   with them?   Yes   No   ? or NA
10. smile freely and often?   Yes   No   ? or NA
11. use good telephone techniques?   Yes   No   ? or NA
12. act sensitive to timing and follow up
    with you?   Yes   No   ? or NA
13. appropriately touch you (a hand-
    shake, pat on back, etc.)?   Yes   No   ? or NA
14. seem to enjoy people and their
    diversity?   Yes   No   ? or NA
15. seem to have good attitudes about
    selling?   Yes   No   ? or NA
16. keep the work place clean and
    attractive?   Yes   No   ? or NA
17. dress and groom themselves
    appropriately?   Yes   No   ? or NA
18. seem to enjoy working for this
    company?   Yes   No   ? or NA

Part II. Customer Loyalty Index

1. Overall, how satisfied were you with [name of company or
   organization]?

   | Extremely unsatisfied | Unsatisfied | Neutral | Satisfied | Extremely satisfied |

2. How likely would you be to recommend [name of company or
   organization] to a friend or associate?

   | Very unlikely | Not likely | Maybe | Very likely | Certain |

3. How likely are you to do business with [name of company or
   organization] again?

   | Very unlikely | Not likely | Maybe | Very likely | Certain |

Scoring: For Part I of the interview, the behaviors, score one point for
each "yes" response. Total possible = 18

For the CLI, score each item on a five-point scale from left to right
(e.g., the most negative response is a 1, the most positive a 5, and
those in between 2, 3, or 4.)

After you have tallied scores for your entire sample (minimum of

10) write a brief analysis of the results. Comment especially on the behaviors that most seem to relate to customer loyalty, as your customers see them.

NOTES

[1] Berry, D. "Booth Won't Take Toll, but Bad Attitude Will," Knight-Ridder Newspapers, April 7, 1991. Reprinted with permission.

[2] Many of the ideas in this section are adapted from Timm, P., *50 Powerful Ideas You Can Use to Keep Your Customers* 2nd ed., (Hawthorne, NJ: Career Press, 1995). Copyright Paul R. Timm.

[3] Decker, B. *The Art of Communication* (Menlo Park, CA: Crisp Publications, 1988), p. 17.

[4] An excellent 30-minute videotape training program featuring the author is *Winning Telephone Techniques* produced by JWA Video in Chicago. For information, call 312-829-5100.

[5] These ideas are found in Chapman, E. N., *The Fifty Minute Sales Training Program* (Menlo Park, CA: Crisp Publications, 1992).

[6] "A Picnic in a Car Lot?" in *Wall Street Journal*, October 13, 1994, p. A-1.

[7] Excerpted from "Banks hang up on pesky customers," in *Kiplinger's Personal Finance Magazine*, August 1996, pp.84–85. Reprinted with permission of The Kiplinger Washington Editors, Inc.

[8] Richards, D., "Sour Smell of Poor Customer Service," *Wall Street Journal*, December 28, 1992, p. A-10. Reprinted with permission.

The Role
of the Supervisor,
Manager, or Leader
Successfully herding cats!

Employees tend to live up to—or down to—their manager's expectations of them.

—Management axiom

THE WAY IT IS . . .

A recent national news magazine carried a letter from a reader who was responding to a story critical of the poor service given by a large retailer. This retailer had seen its profits fall dramatically. The reader said:

> I found [the story] extremely timely and on the mark. Having spent the past 20 years in sales and marketing, 10 of them in discount and upscale retail management, I still can't decide if the [Company's] posture has been one of "you snooze, you lose" or simple corporate arrogance. Perhaps [company] may just now be waking up to the fact that you can no longer abuse your customers and get away with it. Your article spoke of [an] example where only four checkout lanes out of 12 were open. We also see four checkout lanes open, with a dozen customers in each lane, the manager on duty and head cashier standing with arms crossed at the service desk surveying the chaos. On one trip, when I asked the manager why he didn't either open a register himself or bag items for the checkers, he responded that it wasn't his job.

My heart goes out for the well-being of the quality folks who work at the stores. Regardless of their efforts, they can only raise the level of quality up to that point "allowed" by the corporate structure and support mechanisms.[1]

Is this reader fair in placing the blame for poor service on management? This chapter will consider that question as we examine the roles of managers and leaders in providing customer service.

-------------------- *Learning Objectives* --------------------

After you have studied this chapter, you should be able to:

1. Describe the basic functions of management.

2. Recognize that the central thread running through all management functions is communication and that organizations suffer when communication is ineffective.

3. Lead the process of creating an effective customer service credo or theme.

4. Set objectives and develop an effective customer satisfaction strategy.

5. Identify some potentially disquieting (yet penetrating) questions that readily point to customer service problems.

6. Manage the service process with questions.

7. Instruct and motivate employees to provide quality customer service.

8. Identify and implement the seven critical tasks to initiate and sustain an E-Plus customer loyalty strategy.

9. Describe and apply the TQM-TQS model for process improvement.

WHAT MANAGERS, SUPERVISORS, OR LEADERS DO

Many readers of this book are preparing for or are currently in management positions in organizations. By management positions I am referring to any situation where a person supervises or leads the efforts of others. (I'll use variations of the term "manage" to keep things simple.) How do management responsibilities affect the need for customer service skills? The manager's job calls for an ability to get others to do the right things in addition to doing the right things oneself. The ability to multiply one's efforts explains why managers are typically paid more and why skilled managers are always in demand. Their impact on an organization cannot be overvalued.

Managing can be like herding cats!

The Functions of Management

The manager's job consists of four key functions: planning, organizing, commanding or coordinating, and controlling. Let's look at each function as it might relate to customer service.

1. *Planning* is a thinking process—a sort of internal communication within one's mind. The manager looks ahead to what must be done to maintain and improve performance, to solve problems, and to develop employee competence. To plan, a manager sets objectives in each area that is to be pursued this week, this month, this year. Having set these objectives, the manager then thinks through such questions as:
   - What has to be done to reach these objectives?
   - How will these activities be carried out?
   - Who will do them?
   - When will these activities take place?
   - Where will this work be done?
   - What resources will be needed?

        Such planning involves asking questions of customers, both internal and external, and determining what to do in the future based on the input received.

   > Effective planning involves gathering information and projecting future outcomes.

2. *Organizing* involves arranging the work sequence and assigning areas of responsibility and authority. Having decided the objectives and activities of the work unit, the manager must:
   - Assign these responsibilities to employees.
   - Give employees the supporting authority to fulfill their responsibilities.

Much of this work involves reducing potential problems caused by systems (staffing, training, work layout, etc.). Remember that "systems" involve anything having to do with the delivery of products or services to the customer. Constantly organizing and improving systems is a major leadership responsibility.

> The management responsibility for systems improvement often involves organizing.

3. The principles of *commanding* and *coordinating* are often summed up in the term *leading*. The manager leads by enabling the organization to achieve its objectives. To do this, he or she:

- Shows the direction in which subordinates must go.
- Generates the energy (motivation) that subordinates must feel.
- Provides the needed resources to accomplish the tasks.

Modern management emphasizes the motivation aspects of this function. An organization's leaders set the tone for motivation throughout. Motivation can be simply defined as "providing motives for action." Leaders provide motives or reasons why people should act in particular ways.

4. *Controlling* is the function of ensuring that employees are working toward the selected objectives. It involves comparing actual results to expected or planned-for results so as to identify any deviation from plan. Typically, any deviation from plan calls for adjusting motivation attempts, replanning of activities so as to close the gap, or changing the objectives to be more realistic.

> Controlling is a process of following up to be certain that planned for actions are, in fact, being carried out. Managers inspect what they expect.

THE COMMON THREAD IN MANAGEMENT FUNCTIONS

Each of these management functions involves *people*. Herein lies the universal characteristic of the manager's job: Only when managers *accomplish work with and through other people* are they doing the job correctly.

To ensure smooth functioning of any organization, managers must maintain an ongoing flow of appropriate communication. Below are some ways poor communication can damage organizational results. Careful managers work to overcome these kinds of problems.

> The essence of the manager's job is to accomplish work with and through other people.

THREE WAYS ORGANIZATIONS SUFFER FROM POOR COMMUNICATION

Organizational failures occur when too little communication takes place, too much communication is attempted, or ineffective communication is widespread. Let's consider each of these conditions.

Too Little Communication

Crumbling relationships and dysfunctional families often result from too little communication. Countless marriages fail primarily because of couples withhold expressions of appreciation, concern, or ideas. People who cannot express their feelings to each other in marriage seldom succeed as a family organization.

Likewise, businesses where customers are not asked about their needs, where employees have insufficient product knowledge, or employees don't know what behaviors are appropriate, run a huge risk of internal confusion and poor service success. Good organizations keep their people well trained and fully informed. Great organizations constantly solicit information from stake holders (all people who share an interest in the company's success) and act upon it.

> Keeping people informed and getting a constant flow of information from stake holders are characteristics of strong organizations.

Too Much Communication

People who find themselves bombarded with too much information, much of it irrelevant, may collapse under the load. This is the organizational equivalent of the old quip: "I asked him what time it was and he told me how to build a watch." Smart companies keep people informed of things they need to know or may want to know, but don't bombard them with trivia.

> Communication overload can cripple an organization and damage employee productivity.

Widespread Ineffective Communication

Widespread ineffective communication also results in organizational failure for several reasons. Among the most common are unclear direction or coordination, inadequate processing of important data, and missed organizational opportunities. Some examples of ineffective communication may be overuse of poorly planned meetings, failure to publicize accomplishments, poor telephone techniques, or ineffective writing.

PEOPLE PREFER TO DO BUSINESS WITH ORGANIZATIONS THAT COMMUNICATE WELL

I've asked thousands of people at training sessions to think about places they regularly do business and then asked for specific reasons why they kept going back. In every group I'd get responses like these:

- The waitresses (or proprietors or clerks) are really friendly. They call me by name and seem genuinely interested in me.
- Old Phil at the gas station waves when I drive by.
- The butcher Mike listens to me when I ask for a special cut of meat.
- Sarah's so friendly—she's always willing to help.
- Doc Peterson's nurses are really nice. They seem to take a real interest in the kids.

The words are different, but the theme is almost always the same: The organization, through its people, *communicates* a sense of caring. Conversely, studies conducted by the Forum Corporation interviewed customers lost in business-to-business relationships (one business buying from another). The research concluded that 69 percent of those business customers who stopped buying were lost not because of product quality or cost, but because they felt badly treated.[2]

> The greatest cause of lost customers: they feel badly treated.

When we asked people what organizations they "hate to do business with?" respondents often cite government agencies or departments within a company whose people convey a sense that "You [the customer] are an intrusion," "We really don't care whether you are satisfied or not," "I hate my job and it's partly your fault," or "I can't be bothered with you now." They don't say these things out loud, of course, but they do convey these impressions.

> A lack of caring is clearly communicated, even if not in words.

An obvious and significant challenge for managers is to be sensitive to the ways their employees communicate to the world around them—especially customers.

THE MESSAGE RECEIVER DETERMINES COMMUNICATION SUCCESS

Another point about the nature of communication is important: *we really can't control communication*. We can, and must, seek to influence it, but ultimately it is the message receiver (customer) who determines the meaning. This is a frustrating state of affairs for people who have a simplified view of what it means to communicate.

> Although we cannot ultimately control communication, we can learn effective ways to influence it.

Communicating with another person is not a science; it is an art. No magic checklist of precise and exacting procedures exists. Specific, sound principles and themes can be learned but there are thousands of variations on these themes.

Developing the art of communication often means letting go of old assumptions and getting out of the comfortable rut of communicating as usual. Improvement has little to do with talking louder, more emphatically, or more earnestly. It has little to do with increasing the amount of information we project to others. It has little to do with making the message sound better and better to us. It has everything to do with *developing more understanding*. This means looking at the world through the eyes of others, walking the proverbial mile in another's moccasins. Most of us are hesitant to do this, but it is exactly through this kind of empathizing that meaningful improvement of communication occurs.

THE MANAGING FUNCTIONS IN CUSTOMER SERVICE

Let's take a closer look at key management functions and identify some specific actions we can take to work with and through other people to create customer satisfaction and loyalty.

Planning for Better Service: Articulating a Theme

The planning function includes management efforts to articulate a vision forecasting where the organization would like to go. One idea found useful for many organizations is to develop a service theme or credo. Some call it a mission statement.

As I consult with organizations, I typically ask if they have a customer service theme or credo. Fairly often I get answers something like this: "Oh, yes, we have 13 points to excellent customer service."

I'd reply, "Oh, really? What's point 11?" and the manager would say, "Well, I don't know exactly." Then I'd ask, "Well, how about point six? Which one's that?" And again the typical answer is, "I'm not sure, I actually haven't memorized all these things, but we have these points posted in every store."

Unfortunately, that doesn't do much good. To articulate a theme means to come up with a succinct, clear statement of what the organization is about and how it could be seen as unique in the eyes of the customer.

Let's go through that one more time. An effective service theme must be:

- succinct
- clear
- descriptive of uniqueness

One writer says one criteria for a good mission statement or theme is that "You could repeat it at gunpoint!"[3]

The reason you want it succinct and clear is so that every employee can remember and "buy into" this as a guiding statement that will shape their actions and help them make decisions. Let's look at a couple of examples.

One well-respected customer service organization is Federal Express, the package delivery service. Do they have a simple, clear theme? I think they do. In fact, they express it in three words: "Absolutely, positively, overnight." They will get the packages there absolutely, positively, overnight, and they're 99.8 percent successful at doing that. The direct marketing clothier, Lands End has a simple motto/credo that has just two words: "Guaranteed. Period." Both of these themes communicate the company's highest customer-service priority.

A *Harvard Business Review*[4] article told of a Seattle restaurant staff who wrestled with this idea of a simple, clear theme. After carefully looking at the company through the eyes of their customer—just what does our restaurant guest want from us?—they came up with this theme: "Your enjoyment guaranteed. Always." That is exactly what they offer their guests, enjoyment.

A neat thing about this simple theme was that people could buy into it, and in fact they made it into an acronym: YEGA. While YEGA may not mean anything to most of us, it became a catch word for their organization. They developed YEGA promotions and YEGA bucks and YEGA pins and hats to get their employees involved in the spirit of YEGA. It was fun, it was interesting, and it reminded the employees constantly of that simple four-word theme: "Your enjoyment guaranteed. Always."

Here is what managers can do to articulate a good theme.

- *Commit* to work on the process of identifying a theme that is *succinct, clear and descriptive* of your uniqueness.
- *Gather ideas from your customers (internal and external)*. Ask them, "What five things do you want as customers in doing business with us?" Ask them to respond quickly off the tops of their heads, and look at the language that they use.

- Similarly, gather your own people together in the organization and ask, *"If you were our customer, what five things would you like to get from a company like ours?"* Ask people to respond quickly. Jot down the language and then collect all of the words.

As you gather perceptions from customers and employees, you'll notice that some terms come up over and over again. These typically are the kinds of words that will reassure your customer. These are good words to put into your customer service theme.

> Listen for key words from customers as you develop a theme.

As you draft a theme for your organization, remember:

- Participation and input from customers and employees is very important. The customers can best tell you what they're looking for in an organization like yours, and the employees' participation will ensure that they will accept and, hopefully, live by the intention of the theme.
- Write several rough drafts of the theme; don't be too quick to come up with the finished version. Phrase the final version in 10 words or fewer.
- If possible, try to make the theme into an acronym, where the first letters of each word form a word in themselves. The YEGA example given earlier is such an acronym.

When you've identified a statement of uniqueness, ask yourself the question: Would everyone in the organization choose roughly the same words you chose to describe this distinctiveness? A simple way to verify this is to grab some of your employees and ask them to describe the organization's theme. Especially invite an employee who's been with the organization for 10 days or less to identify the theme.

What good does it do just to be able to repeat such a phrase? The answer is that it's a start. Repeating some words may seem meaningless at first, but most organizations fall far short of even that level of agreement. Focusing your people on a common theme can be well worth the effort.

One final note: A theme is not necessarily forever. As an organization changes directions, as markets or economic conditions change, a theme may be modified. Some organizations may want to use a theme statement for a limited period of time much the way advertisers use a slogan for only a few years. Modifying the theme should not, however, be done without careful thought. Consistency of direction is in itself valuable.

> Be sure to involve employees and customers in developing a service theme.

Important: By having employees participate in clarifying a theme, they will feel more committed to it. This has been shown time and again since the earliest studies in human relations. Front-line people know the customers best and can give great ideas on how to better serve them. Never overlook the ideas of this group of experts. The employees on the firing line have the best ideas. Use them.

SETTING OBJECTIVES AND DEVELOPING A SERVICE STRATEGY

The next management planning function involves determining desired service end results and deciding how and when to achieve service goals. Goal setting has long been recognized as a powerful tool for focusing effort. Be sure that targeted improvements are measurable and reasonable. Changes in organizational behaviors and results take time. Don't rush the process. Goal setting helps establish priorities, sequence, and timing of strategy steps. You can't fix everything at once, so look for the kinds of results that can give you the most impact relative to the effort involved. Pick the low hanging fruit first. Handling the obvious shortcomings can motivate the troops to tackle the more difficult problems later.

Managers typically need to budget for improvements. Many changes, especially those that attack systems or value turnoffs, require the expenditure of money or other resources. Once better methods are developed, establish them as policy—as standing decisions on how the organization is to work. Later in this chapter you'll find a seven-step process for creating an ongoing strategy.

ORGANIZE PEOPLE AND DELINEATE AUTHORITY

The organizing function of management involves such actions as clarifying the organizational structure, assigning certain responsibilities, and giving authority to organization members. People at all levels need to know the scope and range of their jobs. Employees need to understand what they can or cannot do for the customer.

Among companies giving legendary service, people at all levels are given a lot of latitude. Nordstrom employees know they can do almost anything to meet a customer's needs. They have been known to send clothing to customers using overnight delivery (regardless of the additional cost) and to give customers an add-on to recompense for any customer disappointment. Ritz Carlton hotel employees are encouraged to take personal "ownership" for any problem a guest may have. If a guest's need comes to their attention, they drop what they are doing and solve the problem or meet the guest's need. Bellhops have been known to rush out of the hotel to buy a foreign newspaper for a guest who was disappointed that the publication wasn't available in the hotel's gift shop. No questions asked, managers have given bellhops the authority to do whatever it takes. This may be one reason that Ritz Carlton won the prestigious Baldridge Award for corporate excellence.

STAFF WITH QUALITY EMPLOYEES

Managers are responsible for recruiting qualified people for each employee position, orienting new people to the company's service expectations, and providing training so that people become proficient by instruction and practice.

Some successful managers recruit by stealing good employees from other companies. (That statement may be a bit too strong, but the principle works.) As managers come across people with great attitudes and excellent customer service skills, they might try to hire them away or at least recommend them to company recruiters.

One owner of a chain of fast food restaurants solved his problem of getting quality people in a high-turnover industry by giving his business card to employees of other companies who wait on him. He'd say something like, "Thank you for your great service. You did a nice job. If you are ever interested in changing jobs, I'd appreciate it if you'd call me personally. I'm sure I could find a place for you in my organization."

An ongoing process should be to keep a file of people you'd like to have working for you and when an opening occurs, contact them. Don't worry if they are working in a totally different type of business. The specifics of your organization can be taught. Great attitudes cannot.

Once hired, managers need to be sure that people have ample opportunity to develop their knowledge, attitudes, and skills. The best jobs are those that allow people to grow.

DIRECTING THE COMPANY'S EFFORTS

Managers fulfill their directing functions by delegating. This means assigning responsibility and accountability for service results to the people they manage. They also need to motivate by persuading and inspiring people to take desired action. Other directing functions include coordinating desired efforts in the most efficient combination, managing differences, resolving conflicts, and stimulating creativity and innovation in achieving service goals.

CONTROLLING THE ORGANIZATION

Managers need to determine what critical service data are needed to track important results. They can then measure key results and compare them with the goals or standards. Control also involves taking corrective action by coaching people to help them attain standards or by adjusting the plan as needed. Finally, providing rewards is a crucial part of controlling and motivating.

Managers have a lot to do, as you can see.

SOME POTENTIALLY DISQUIETING QUESTIONS MANAGERS NEED TO ANSWER

A starting point for determining how well an organization is doing with customer service may be to answer questions like the ones below. A positive response to one or more of these may not be devastating, but if you answer yes to most of them, your organization is likely to face an uphill battle in attempting to substantially improve customer service:

Does your company, organization, or department . . .

1. Talk about customer service but pay front-line people a low, flat wage?
2. Offer little or no training in fundamentals of customer service for customer contact people?
3. Offer no special incentives for taking care of the customer?
4. Punish or reprimand employees poor customer service but take good service for granted?
5. Place greater emphasis on winning new customers than retaining ones it already has?
6. Offer no awards or recognition for non-customer contact people's efforts to serve?
7. Hold "be nice to the customer" programs or campaigns that last for a few weeks or months but are soon forgotten?
8. Have top managers who rarely if ever devote time to listening to customers and helping them solve problems?
9. Make no effort to measure service quality as perceived by customers?
10. Make no attempt to hold managers at all levels accountable for and rewarded on the basis of service?

Most managers would have to answer "yes" to several of the above questions. That, in itself, is not an indicator of poor service policies, but it could point to some potential problem areas. And the process of asking lots of penetrating questions can be a valuable management activity.

HOW TO MANAGE WITH QUESTIONS

Author Bill Maynard[5] agrees that the art of management often involves asking lots of questions. He recommends that as managers interact with people throughout the organization as well as with customers, they ask questions like these:

- What made you mad today?
- What took too long?
- What caused complaints today?
- What was misunderstood today?
- What costs too much?

- What was too complicated?
- What was just plain silly?
- What job involved too many people?
- What job involved too many actions?
- What was wasted?

An effective manager would be wise to commit these questions to memory and ask them often. Then, of course, it is crucial that they act on the answers people give to the degree possible.

Self-Analysis

Understand Your Feedback Receptiveness Attitude

Think back to the last time you received criticism from someone else. Recall a specific event or situation. Describe it in a few sentences. Now, mentally review the situation. To what degree did you:

1. Hold back on defending or explaining yourself until the full criticism was fully expressed?
2. Work to understand to critiquer's point of view as best you could?
3. Ask for elaboration or clarification without being overly defensive?
4. Express an honest reaction?
5. Thank the person for the feedback?

For most people, *giving* criticism (even in a constructive way) is risky. When people first offer such feedback, they watch closely to gauge the receiver's responses. The reaction they receive will usually determine whether they will offer feedback again. This means that *you* have the opportunity to avoid turning off future feedback that could be valuable to you.

Overall, how would you rate your feedback attitude in the above situation? What might you change, if anything?

INSTRUCTING AND MOTIVATING EMPLOYEES

"Management by walking around" has, in recent years, been seen as an increasingly important function of the manager. Doing so increases opportunities for giving recognition and gaining insights from the people "on

Reprinted with special permission of King Features Syndicate.

the firing line." The payoff goes beyond mere pleasant interpersonal relations; it shows up in better motivation and clearer communication among organization members.

A manager can have a profound effect on his or her employees by simply thanking or complimenting them. It sounds simplistic, but the fact remains that, as Robert Townsend said in *Up the Organization*, "Thanks [are] a really neglected form of compensation."[6]

EXPRESSING APPROVAL AND WORKER MOTIVATION

Management consultants have applied systematic approaches to expressing verbal approval that have demonstrated remarkable results. What is a *systematic* approach to expressing verbal approval? The most common one is based in a psychological approach called *behavior modification*.

Managers typically implement such a systematic program by first, holding a series of meetings in which managers and employees discuss mutual needs and problems as well as potential solutions. Key data are "bench-marked," to measure a starting point. These diagnostic sessions provide a base for determining job performance standards and how they will be met. The meetings also identify rewards that managers may use to "modify" the employees' behavior.

The second step is to arrange for worker performance to be observed with a reliable follow-up; the third is to give feedback often, immediately letting employees know how their current level of performance compares with the level desired. For example, in one early attempt, an airline company with five telephone reservation offices employing about 1,800 people kept track of the percentage of calls in which callers make flight reservations. Then they fed back the results daily to each employee. At the same time, supervisors were instructed to praise employees for asking callers for their reservations. Within a few months, the ratio of sales to calls soared from one in four to one in two.[7] It was as simple as counting how often employees asked for the customer's business.

WHY THIS WORKS: A PSYCHOLOGY OF CHANGE

At the heart of any such performance improvement effort is the premise that *future behavior is influenced by the outcomes of past behavior.* If the outcome immediately following an act is in some way rewarding, people are likely to repeat the behavior. If the response is punishing, people are likely not to do it again.

Managers, then, can provide three types of communicated responses to employee behaviors. The normal effects of each response on employee behavior are shown in the right column below.

- Positive reinforcement   encourages employee to repeat the behavior
- Negative reinforcement   encourages employee to avoid the behavior in the future
- No observable response at all   usually causes the employee to extinguish the behavior (no incentive for continuing is given)

Some people question just how far we can go with verbal approval as a motivator. Theoretically, it should work indefinitely as long as appropriate *schedules of reinforcement* are used. The two main reinforcement schedules are *continuous* and *intermittent*. Continuous reinforcement means the individual receives reinforcement (a compliment or supportive statement) every time he or she engages in the desired behavior. This approach is useful when the person is being taught a new behavior and needs to be shored up to develop confidence in this new ability. People learn very quickly, at least initially, under continuous reinforcement.

> Continuous reinforcement gets quick performance results initially.

You can readily see the results of continuing reinforcement when teaching a small child how to do something like catching a ball. If, each time the ball is caught, you praise the child, the child will develop this skill very quickly. The principle generally holds for employees working on unfamiliar tasks.

Yet the use of continuous reinforcement poses at least three problems:

1. It takes too much time, and it therefore costs a great deal in terms of supervisory effort. It is just not feasible always to be there complimenting each job well done—you might as well do the job yourself!
2. It can diminish in effectiveness because of "inflation." Verbal approval can be cheapened by overuse.
3. Once continuous reinforcement is expected, it is tough to wean people away from it without certain risks. If we suddenly drop continuous reinforcement—that is, we no longer express verbal approval for each good behavior—the message to our worker may be that the behavior is no longer appropriate and should be stopped. In short, we may extinguish the desired behavior.

The drawbacks to continuous reinforcement are largely overcome by shifting to *intermittent reinforcement*. Here, instead of expressing approval of every act, we use another system to allocate compliments. We may decide to express approval at intervals, such as each time a particular type of task is completed, say a difficult customer is recovered.

Another intermittent reinforcement approach is to provide rewards at completely random times. Much of the lure of slot-machine gambling comes from the anticipated random windfall. The anticipation or hope of a sudden big reward keeps the players engaged in the "desired behavior"—putting money in the slot. Random rewarding with unexpected bonuses can have this effect.

> Random, intermittent reinforcement can lead to longer term motivation.

Under random intermittent reinforcement the worker doesn't know exactly when he or she will be rewarded. So long as the employee holds hope of eventually receiving a reward such as verbal approval, extinction of desired behavior is delayed. If the rewards are too far apart, of course, the worker will not continue to produce unless he or she is particularly good at working hard today for some far-off, but certain-to-be-worthwhile reward. Relatively few workers today are content to "get their reward in heaven."

The best approach is to use continuous reinforcement when new behaviors are being developed and then gradually move to an intermittent schedule so the desired performance won't be inadvertently extinguished. In other words, shift the employees' expectations so that longer intervals between reinforcement are seen as normal.

PRAISE AND CRITICISM

Sometimes praise is downright embarrassing and so-called constructive criticism just plain makes you mad. Morrison and O'Hearne have developed an explanation of why praise and criticism seem to have such an on-again-off-again value.[8] These authors suggest that both praise and criticism can be broken down into two types. Type 1 praise consists of those statements that have little effect on the performance of the receiver. They roll away like water off a duck's back. Type 2 praise consists of those statements that *might* have a positive effect on performance under certain circumstances. There are no guarantees, but these kinds of "attaboys" and "attagirls" might motivate or at least build stronger relationships between the giver and the receiver. Some examples of Type 1 and Type 2 praise are offered in Figure 6-1.[9]

A similar classification of criticism is illustrated in Figure 6-2. Type 1 criticism results in defensiveness and deterioration of performance while Type 2 criticism is at least potentially constructive in that it *might* result in improved future performance.[10]

Figure 6–1 Ineffective versus Effective Praise

Type 1 praise—has little effect on performance of the receiver.	Type 2 praise—may have a positive effect on performance and build an authentic relationship.
1. Generalized praise such as, "You're doing a good job, Charlie." This is meaningless and it generally rolls off the back of the individual without effect. It is often seen as a "crooked" stroke.	1. Specific praise—such as, "Charlie, you did a great job handling that unpleasant customer with a complaint this afternoon." This communicates to the receiver that the boss has actually observed or heard about the praised action.
2. Praise with no further meaning. There is no analysis of why a praised behavior is being commended. This discounts the persons being praised by assuming they will react with higher productivity and better morale merely as a response.	2. Continuing with, "The reason I think it was such a good job is because you acted interested, asked questions, wrote down the facts, asked the customer what she thought we should do to make it right." Analysis of this kind permits the employee to internalize the learning experience.
3. Praise for expected performance, when such praise may be questioned. Mabel, who always gets in on time and is met one morning with, "Mabel, you're sure on time today, you're doing great," from her boss, may wonder what's really going on.	3. Praise for better-than-expected results, for coming in over quota, exceeding the target, putting out extra effort.
4. The "sandwich" system—praise is given first to make the person be receptive to criticism (the real reason for the transaction), which is then followed by another piece of praise, hoping, thereby to encourage the person to try harder next time, feel better about the criticism.	4. Praise, when deserved, is believable when it is given by itself; when mixed with critique it is suspect. Authentic relations develop better when people talk straight. When positive conditional recognition is in order, give it; when critique is deserved, give that. Don't mix the two.
5. Praise perceived by the receiver as given in the nature of a "carrot," mainly to encourage the receiver to work even harder in the future.	5. Praise that is primarily to commend and recognize, and does not seek to put a mortgage on the future.
6. Praise handed out lavishly only when the brass or higher-ups are present. Employees soon recognize the boss is trying to impress superiors with what a good human being he or she really is in dealing with subordinates.	6. Praise given when it is deserved, not just on special occasions, when it seems to build the image of the praiser to some third party.

Figure 6–2 Destructive versus Constructive Criticism

Type 1 criticism—tends to produce a defensive reaction in the receiver and worsen performance.	Type 2 criticism—a type of constructive criticism that may improve performance.
1. Criticism that involves use of the personal "you," e.g., "You're having too many accidents on the lift truck, Bill. What's the matter with you anyway?" It is almost always seen as a discount or put-down by the receiver.	1. Criticism using a situational description, e.g., "Bill, we're experiencing an increase in lift-truck accidents. What's going on?" This indicates the manager is open to looking at all the facts leading to the unfavorable result.
2. Criticism that is unanalyzed. The subordinate then tends to rationalize the criticism as a personal opinion of the manager. Or, the manager is viewed as unable to analyze the problems effectively.	2. Discussion of cause and effect with the unfavorable condition perceived by both as the result of one or more causal factors, one of which might even be the manager!
3. If the situation has been properly assessed, some managers are at a loss to provide coaching necessary for the subordinate to improve. This may be the result of ignorance or lack of competency in deciding on the corrective steps.	3. If steps 1 and 2 above have been properly accomplished, it is important for solutions to be outlined and agreed on. If the subordinate can't do this, the manager must provide, or arrange, for a resource that can develop corrective measures.
4. Critique of an individual in public is not only regarded as humiliating by the subordinate involved, but sometimes even more so by other members of the organization.	4. Individual criticism given in private is usually more acceptable. Saving face is almost as important in Western cultures as it is in the Orient.
5. Criticism given *only* in the interests of the boss (to get the boss recognition, promotion, or raise) or the organization (more profit or status in the marketplace). These may all be legitimate interests, but *authentic* relationships are not likely to develop.	5. Criticism given *also*, or even chiefly, in the interests of the employee (to provide greater competencies, future achievements, or a more secure future with the organization).
6. The manager does all the critiquing which sets the stage for a Parent-Child [relationship].	6. The subordinate participates in the critiques, even to the point of taking the lead role in defining the unsatisfactory condition, analyzing causes, and suggesting corrective steps.
7. Criticism used as a [calculated] game to justify withholding raises or promotions.	7. Game-free criticism leading toward candor and [authentic interactions].

GIVING INSTRUCTIONS

Often the most frequent communications managers have with employees is giving orders, directions, or instructions. Although some bosses think of this as one-way, boss-to-subordinate communication, a two-way format is usually far more appropriate.

> Two-way instruction giving works best.

As managers, we need to know exactly what action we want to result from instructions given. That seems self-evident. Yet this step is occasionally overlooked. When we give an employee instructions to "be more responsive to customers," we may not have a clear picture of exactly what behavior we want to see. Instead we need to mentally clarify our purpose—our reason for giving the order—and then *plan* the best way of creating understanding with the employee.

The phrase "be more responsive" will likely have different meanings for different people. An effective instruction-giver will create a clearer picture of what he wants by supplying some details, such as, "you need to greet each customer within ten seconds when they come into the store."

> Use clear, concrete terms when giving instructions.

Providing sufficient details and *repetition* are good ways to minimize misunderstandings. The journalist's "who, what, where, when, why, and how" provide a good framework for giving instructions. Be sure you know the answers to each of these before directing someone else. And be sure to encourage questions from the message receiver.

Asking "Do you have any questions?" probably isn't the best technique. The question calls for a yes-or-no response, and many people opt for "no" to avoid showing ignorance. By changing the wording to "What questions do you have?" you say to the employee "It's okay to have questions" and you encourage task clarification. Be sure to pause long enough to let your listeners know you are serious about getting questions from them.

HOW MANAGERS CAN INITIATE AND SUSTAIN AN E-PLUS CUSTOMER LOYALTY STRATEGY[11]

Managers can "operationalize" good intentions into a workable E-Plus strategy by implementing seven key tasks described briefly below. These need not always be done in the order presented, but several will be done concurrently.

TASK #1: Orient All Employees

Take steps to insure that all employees clearly understand the need for cultivating customer loyalty. Teach them about the cost of lost customers, how lost customers lead to lost jobs, why poor service givers pay a psychological price, and why it is in their best interest to develop customer-service professionalism. This step is typically done via a series of training sessions.

Also, through training, strive to get employees speaking the same language. Be sure they know the importance of little things, service attitudes, E-Plus and VISPAC, for example.

Begin any strategy by orienting employees.

TASK #2: Build Momentum

Conduct regular follow-up departmental meetings after the initial training. Teach basic creativity and group problem-solving skills, schedule and conduct regular brainstorming sessions to discuss possible new E-plus ideas. Show individuals and work groups how to set departmental or team goals.

Coordinate a reward system so that the most useful activities get the best rewards. Create a reward committee to determine special bonuses, determine budget, define criteria whereby people can win the rewards. Then develop data-gathering forms/processes that give credit for good works. Distribute "Attaboy, Attagirl" cards or small rewards to recognize success immediately.

TASK #3: Monitor Customer Expectation and Employee Behavior

Teach "naive listening" techniques to employees. Recognize the value of unhappy customers as sources of improvement ideas. Schedule focus groups, regularly—on the calendar. Record, digest, and keep data and trends analysis.

At the same time, conduct regular shopper surveys to determine the kinds of service people are getting from employees. These should typically be done by independent "shopper services" that provide immediate and specific feedback to employees.

TASK #4: Establish Systematic Customer Retention/Follow-up Efforts

Develop creative customer follow-up techniques. Schedule regular follow-ups with mailouts, phone calls, announcements, and special incentives. Try other loyalty builders such as customer photos or customer letters posted on display. Perhaps establish a "Customer of the Month " recognition.

TASK #5: Provide Continuation Training for Employees

Schedule repeat "basic" training for new employees. Also schedule regular continuation training where employees can receive instruction on tasks such as writing customer correspondence, handling difficult people, improving telephone techniques, time and task management, etc.

TASK #6: Conduct Ongoing Systems Reviews

Create a task force to review systems. Employ explorer groups to visit competitors or similar businesses which have good ideas. Create a suggestion program to improve systems by announcing and publicizing it, budgeting award money, creating forms, and forming a review committee to evaluate suggestions submitted.

TASK #7: Recruit, Develop, and Retain Excellent Employees

Attract and select exceptional service personnel by developing aptitude/attitude testing and interviewing procedures. Proactively invite promising employees from other businesses to join you.

Once hired, be sure to clarify promotion criteria and tie these criteria to the customer-service reward system. In short, base employee advancement on service attitudes and skills. As part of this process, be sure to conduct meaningful performance reviews with service criteria being measured and factored into review.

CUSTOMER STRATEGY AND CONTINUOUS IMPROVEMENT

Customer satisfaction and loyalty present moving targets. What may be seen as the latest, greatest service idea today may quickly become passé. A few years ago, price scanners in supermarkets were rare. Today, we expect them. A few years ago, the idea of offering takeout restaurant service was an innovation. Today it's commonplace. The list of service innovations goes on and the good ones quickly become standard operating procedures.

The outcome of raising the bar of customer expectation is that we all get better service. This is good. But it presents yet another challenge for organizations committed to staying on the leading edge.

In the past decade a number of business buzzwords have emerged to describe various processes for continuously improving. "Total Quality Management (TQM)," "Continuous Quality Improvement (CQI)," and a range of similar initialisms were posed as useful procedures for bringing about a constantly improving spiral of product and service quality.

The granddaddy of these approaches is TQM as originally articulated by W. Edwards Deming.[12] In the years following World War II, Deming, an American statistician with a new management theory, took his ideas to Japan. The Japanese, devastated by the effects of the war, were looking to restructure their economy, and Deming's principles became the blueprint they needed. Now, of course, Japanese products are in demand worldwide.

The Japanese success story made Deming's management theory, Total Quality Management (TQM), a phenomenon that got renewed attention in America. With its focus on customer satisfaction, employee empowerment, and product quality, it stirred interest among American managers, from car manufacturers to hospital administrators, and more recently, even educators.

> TQM focuses on customer service, employee empowerment, and product quality.

What Is the Philosophy of TQM?

Although no two businesses use TQM in exactly the same way, its theory rests on two basic tenets. The first and most important is that customers are vital to the operation of the organization. Without customers, there is no business, and without business, there is no organization. Consequently, it should be the primary aim of any group to keep customers satisfied by providing them with quality products.

These ideas are not foreign to most organizations; what makes TQM unique is its second basic tenet: a call for a restructuring of management methods to create that quality. TQM proponents urge organizations to turn nearsighted, top-down management "on its head" by involving both customers and employees in decisions. This second tenet, that management needs to listen to nontraditional sources of information in order to institute quality, is based on the belief that people want to do quality work and that they would do it if managers would listen to them and create a workplace based on their ideas.

Managers, in the TQM view, need to become leaders who not only work *in* the system but also *on* the system. A company will see continuous improvement in products only when managers realize all systems consist of interdependent parts and work to aim all those parts toward a vision of quality, proponents argue. This type of leadership is needed to ensure that product quality improves "constantly and forever" and truly satisfies the customers.

How Does TQM Create an Environment that Promotes Quality?

TQM advocates specific changes that managers need to make if they want to improve their organization's systems. These changes are best described under the four categories below:

- *Customer Relationships:* Customers can be either internal or external to an organization. Just as a customer is the person buying a product in a store, an employee is the customer of management. Managers need to realize that quality work will not be done unless they provide employees with quality products to work with.[13]
- *Employee Empowerment:* TQM starts at the top but should permeate throughout the workplace; in fact, it will fail without employee involvement. Since workers know more about their jobs than management does, their input is vital to improving the system. It is a manager's responsibility to continually train employees in the methods of TQM, involve them in decisions affecting the company, listen to their suggestions for system changes, and work to implement those changes.
- *Continual Gathering and Use of Statistical Data:* Most companies monitor the quality of their products by doing mass inspections that determine how many low-quality items are being produced, but TQM calls for monitoring of the production process by continually gathering statistical data so that problems can be identified as they are happening instead of when it is too late to solve them. When problems are identified, they should be the focus of discussion, and the groups discussing them should rely on the data to institute change instead of randomly assigning blame to individuals or departments.[14]
- *Creating an Environment that Promotes Unity and Change:* People need to feel comfortable discussing problems and suggesting solutions. Managers need to work at breaking down barriers between departments so that interactive discussion can take place. Fear must be eliminated. Also, managers are urged to emphasize teamwork rather than put the focus on competition among individual results.

Cooperative effort is seen as more important than individual competition among employees under TQM.

Service Snapshot

A Fun Way to Start the Week[15]

During her company's Monday morning staff meetings, Susan Groenwald, president of Barter Corp., in Oakbrook Terrace, Ill., asks employees to share examples of exemplary customer service that the company
has provided. Afterward, the 51 workers at the barter network . . . vote
for the example they think had the greatest impact on the company's
customer service. The winner gets either a cash award or bartered
goods. "Rehashing stories gives people a better idea of what good customer service looks like," says Groenwald. "It's also a fun way to start
the week." And there's an additional payoff: the meetings arm the company's salespeople with real-life anecdotes to use when they're wooing
potential clients.

Is TQM a Fad?

The novelty of TQM and the fact that there are so few comprehen-
sive TQM systems have caused many people to label it as a fad. They argue
that TQM, like so many management theories before it, is destined to fade
into obscurity.

Indeed, there is some indication that quality and service improvement is given lip service more often than it is applied. A study for the American Quality Association revealed that despite widespread interest, many
companies have instituted TQM practices without understanding that it
requires a *gradual transformation*. This steady improvement happens only
when an organization's leaders have *long-term vision* and dedication to
systematic change. The primary emphasis in most businesses is still on
short-term profits and individual performance rather than teamwork and
customer satisfaction.[16]

FROM TQM TO TQS: TOTAL QUALITY SERVICE

Building on the basic TQM philosophy, customer service expert Karl
Albrecht describes a model strategy for continuous improvement of customer service which he calls a Total Quality Service (TQS) model[17] (see
Figure 6–3). For each of the elements of Albrecht's original model, I've
added the relevant question we need to ask to institute ongoing service
improvement in an organization.

Figure 6–3 The TQS Model for Total Quality Service
© 1988 Karl Albrecht.

1. Marketing and Customer Research: What Do Our Customers Want?

The starting point of the TQS cycle requires that we know what our customers want. In times past, businesses assumed they knew what customers wanted. Henry Ford offered his Model-T in any color a customer could want so long as it was black. Later, mass marketing polled customer needs and then gave everybody the product that the most people seemed to want. But that was then, this is now. We live in an age where the customer's *individual* wants and needs are considered and acted upon. One large company coined the term "customerize" to allude to its ability to tailor its products to individual customers. (Chapter 9 discusses the future of such personalization)

We've talked about ways to get at customer wants and needs repeatedly in this book. But for a quick review, there are the three most common approaches: fishing for feedback, holding focus groups, and polling customers with comment cards and surveys.

> Successful companies use several techniques to determine what the customer wants.

2. Strategy Formulation: How Can We Best Provide What Customers Want?

The second step of the TQS model points up the need for using input from organization members to develop and refine strategies for meeting—or better yet, exceeding—customer expectations. Our earlier discussion on setting a company-service theme illustrates one way to clarify a commitment to providing our customers with what they want.

Remember that service quality, in the final analysis is determined by the customers. They must be satisfied and remain satisfied if a company is to prosper.

3. Education, Training, and Communication: How Can We Get All Organization Members Involved?

The next step in the TQS model shows a need to train and retrain to build employee competence. People quickly forget ideas conveyed to them in training sessions. Repeated exposures to the same ideas are almost always necessary for people to apply those ideas. Training cannot be a one-shot affair. Training cannot be a once-a-year retreat. Training must be ongoing. It need not always be formal, classroom-style sessions. Often the best training happens in small groups or one-to-one coaching among associates in an organization.

Some supervisors spend about ten minutes each morning before opening to the public to remind service representatives of the skills and behaviors they need to apply. Like a coach warming up a star athlete, the good supervisor will train and retrain on a regular basis.

> Brief coaching or reminder sessions can create training continuity.

Remember, too, that training is much more than just telling. It involves "hands-on" practice, critiques, and regular follow-up.

Sometimes, some good old-fashioned cheerleading works. The legendary Sam Walton would lead cheering sessions at Wal-Mart company meetings. He'd raise his right hand and lead his associates (employees) in the "Sam's Pledge":

> From this day forward, every customer that comes within ten feet of me, regardless of what I'm doing, I'm going to look him in the eye, I'm going to smile, I'm going to greet him with a "Good morning," or "Good afternoon," or a "What can I do for you?"—so help me Sam!

4. Process Improvement: How Can We Consistently Adjust and Improve?

Again, participation, team building, and open communication are crucial to any service improvement process. People at all levels have ideas that can improve processes and services. Companies that open the upward communication channels from employees as well as from external customers will get the most and best improvement ideas.

Since you always get more of what you give, reward good ideas and the willingness to apply the TQS model. Often this reward is nonmonetary. Complimentary letters and memos, recognition announcements, newsletter write-ups, and spoken expressions of appreciation are among the most powerful motivators.

5. Assessment, Measurement, and Feedback: How Can We Tell If We Are Improving?

TQS requires measuring and tracking key figures and observations regarding customer satisfaction. Without ongoing measures and tracking, customer service becomes no more than a short-term "program." Organizations that do track service create the ongoing emphasis needed to achieve competitive advantage.

Among the scores that could be tracked are:

- Average scores received on mystery shoppers surveys. (People posing as customers evaluate the service received.)
- Number of customer complaints received and handled.
- Number of company-initiated calls to customers to assess satisfaction.
- Office accessibility (how many times customers experience a busy signal or long lines).
- Random observations of employee behaviors. Count such things as eye contact time, smiling, efficiency of handling transactions, courtesy, thanking customers, etc.

Businesses must stop measuring performance in financial terms alone. To break the link between service and short-term profitability, "many companies are turning to independent quality audits, and they are reporting the results alongside financial reports to demonstrate success in achieving both profits and quality [service] goals."[18]

The wheel-shape of the TQS Model serves as a reminder that excellence in customer satisfaction is an ongoing process. Thomas Henry Huxley might have been describing a TQS continuous improvement cycle when he said, "The rung of a ladder was never meant to rest upon, but only to hold a man's foot long enough to enable him to put the other somewhat higher."[19]

A FINAL THOUGHT

Managing an organization's customer service is a complex task requiring constant vigilance and effort. Managers can only accomplish their objectives when working with and through the efforts of other people. To do so requires tact and skills in communication and motivation. A key to managerial success is to ask pertinent questions and to be open to feedback. Seven steps to ongoing service improvement provide a way to translate good intentions into a strategy that works.

-------------------- *Summary of Key Ideas* --------------------

- Basic management functions all play a role in creating and sustaining a customer service strategy.
- Communication plays a central role in all management processes. Problems arise when people receive too little, too much, or poorly expressed information.
- Managing functions that can apply to customer service include developing a service theme, setting service goals, delegating responsibility and authority, recruiting good staff, directing actions, and controlling by checking results against goals.
- Managing by asking tough questions can point to weaknesses in any system.
- Employee motivation can be stimulated by systematic rewarding of appropriate behaviors. Among the most powerful motivators is a simple thanks for work well done.
- Praise and criticism must be given judiciously and worded carefully.
- Instructions should be given clearly and repeatedly.
- Seven tasks can effectively translate a slogan into a strategy.
- TQM and its service variation, TQS, can point the way for continuous quality improvement.

Another Look

Peer Coaching: How to Manage when Managers Are Few and Far Between[20]

Once upon a time not very long ago, the average supervisor had responsibility for five to 15 people. In today's world of downsized, re-engineered organizations, that figure is closer to 30. The result is, as one frustrated service manager expressed to me: "We don't do management—we do crowd control."

Yet the need for coaching to achieve high-quality service is greater than ever. The solution of choice: Peer coaching. Employees of the same level, without the traditional leverage of a boss-subordinate relationship, are being asked to coach one another on substandard and problematic performance.

How's it working? It has its enthusiasts and skeptics.

The negatives are easy to imagine. If you've ever been approached by someone offering to "give you a little feedback," you know the potential problems. On the positive side, peers well-trained in the nuances of effective interpersonal communication can be an asset. If you've ever had a colleague pull you aside to warn you the boss is on a tear so you shouldn't bring up the Johnson account, or simply to let you know something was unzipped or stuck between your teeth, you know how valuable peer feedback can be.

Peer coaching—some people prefer to call it peer support—succeeds when the conditions are right and the ground rules clear. Specifically, a successful peer coaching venture requires a supportive environment, awareness of the limits of peer coaching, and tolerance for clumsy communication.

Supportive Environment

If your organization has a history of interdepartmental warfare—marketing and operations only speak through their UN ambassadors, manager-to-manager relations are characterized by jealousy, back-biting and nasty barbs at 20 paces, and employees only hear "well done" when they are ordering steak—then peer coaching will fail in your organization in about 2.5 minutes.

If your organization tolerates mistakes as learning opportunities, not time for punishment, peer coaching has a good chance for success.

Awareness of the Limits

Peer coaching is not a panacea. Rather, it is a way of leveraging your skill as a coach by investing some of it in others. It is a supplement rather than a substitute for the coaching you provide. And it definitely is not a way to get out from under the responsibility of dealing directly with employees who have chronic performance problems. That is never a peer responsibility. Peer coaching—all coaching—is about working together with people to build individual and team success.

There are four fundamental axions to swear allegiance to:

(1) *Peer coaching is not back-seat driving.* Peer coaching is about giving direct, clear feedback and advice, and only doing so with permission or when solicited.

(2) *Peer coaching is not group therapy.* No one in the workplace has a right to probe anyone else's psyche or motivations. The peer coaching process is about "The facts, Ma'am, just the facts." And a limited set of facts—observable, amenable work behavior.

(3) *Helping out is the spirit of peer coaching.* Peer coaching is not a license to blow off steam or give a colleague a piece of your mind. The onus is on the giver to answer three questions before offering Charlie a little help:

- Is Charlie having trouble with a customer, colleague, or situation, or are you uncomfortable with the way Charlie does things?
- Is the problem clearly Charlie's—as opposed to a problem Charlie is involved in but not one he owns?
- If you don't offer to intercede, will the situation cause an irreparable problem for the organization—or for Charlie?

If the answers to all three questions are "yes," you have an obligation to offer help.

Peer coaches respect the "Rule of Once" and the "Right of Refusal":

The Rule of Once: You get to give your feedback and advice once. And only once. The assumption has to be that Charlie heard and understood you. Beyond that he is free to accept, disregard, or hold your input in abeyance.

The Right of Refusal: You and we and Charlie have a right to say "thank you" and ignore peer input. We even have the right to not listen to peer input.

Tolerance for Clumsiness

Giving counsel and advice to a subordinate is a sweaty palms situation for many a seasoned manager. Doing it with a peer is even more tense. So a little tolerance goes a long way in creating a climate where peers can learn to help each other focus their efforts to create a service edge in their organization.

Application Activity
Look Inside at Feedback Receptiveness

Take a moment to answer this short self-quiz. Circle a 5 if the statement is almost always true, a 1 if it's almost never true and some number in between if you prefer to waffle.

A. I feel embarrassed when people point out
   my mistakes.   5 4 3 2 1

B. I resent people telling me what they think
   of my shortcomings.   5 4 3 2 1

C. I regularly ask friends and associates I trust
   to comment on how I am doing.   5 4 3 2 1

D. I know how to offer constructive criticism to
   others in a sensitive way.   5 4 3 2 1

E. I like having people tell me their reactions to
   my activities because it helps me adapt my
   future behavior.   5 4 3 2 1

If you scored 4 or 5 on items A and B, you may be putting up some resistance that could deter you from getting useful feedback. We are normally uncomfortable when we receive harsh or insensitive feedback, but even that can be useful if we wring out the emotion and look at the giver's perspective. Even our worse critic can provide a gift of good advice if we do not allow emotion to blind us. Successful communicators learn to look for good advice even when it's buried under a lot of worthless noise.

If you answered 4 or 5 to items C and D, you are creating a climate where helpful feedback is expected and accepted. People and organizations who foster such openness can benefit from others' advice.

If you answered 4 or 5 to item E, you are probably a little unusual. But you are on the right track.

Remember, being open to feedback does not mean that you necessarily agree with it. But if you get little or no feedback, you have nothing to sort out, apply, or learn from.

NOTES

[1]Nushart, S., letter to the editor, *U.S. News and World Report,* December 11, 1995, p.6.

[2]Whiteley, R. C. *The Customer Driven Company: Moving from Talk to Action* (Reading, MA: Addison-Wesley, 1991), p. 27.

[3]Jones, L. B., *The Path: Creating Your Mission Statement* (New York: Hyperion, 1996), p. 4.

[4]See Firnstahl, T. W., "My Employees Are My Service Guarantee," *Harvard Business Review,* July-August 1989, pp. 28–32.

[5]Maynard, B. "How to Manage with Questions," in *TeleProfessional,* 209 W. 5th Street, Waterloo, IA 50701-5420.

[6]Townsend, R., *Up the Organization* (New York: Knopf, 1970), p. 184.

[7]"Productivity Gains from a Pat on the Back," *Business Week,* January 23, 1978, pp. 57–58.

[8]Morrison, J. H. and O'Hearne, J. H., *Practical Transactional Analysis in Management* (Reading, MA: Addison-Wesley, 1977), pp. 118–121.

[9]Morrison and O'Hearne, pp. 118–119. Reprinted with permission.

[10]Morrison and O'Hearne, pp. 120–121. Reprinted with permission.

[11] This 7-Step Process is © Paul R. Timm, Ph.D. May not be reproduced without written permission. For further information, call Paul R. Timm at (801) 378-5682 or FAX (801) 378-8309 or write to 81 E. 2000 South, Orem, UT 84058 USA.

[12]Excerpted from Weaver, T., "Total Quality Management," *ERIC Digest,* No. 73, ERIC Clearinghouse on Educational Management, Eugene, OR. Office of Educational Research and Improvement (ED), Washington, DC. EDO-EA-92-6 1992 (transmitted via America Online, March 8, 1994.)

[13]Blankstein, A. M. "Lesions from Enlightened Corporations," *Educational Leadership* 49, 6, March 1992, pp. 71–75.

[14]Deming, W. E., *Out of Crisis* (Cambridge, MA: Massachusetts Institute of Technology, 1986).

[15] "Hot Tip," *Inc.* April 1997, p. 95. Reprinted with permission.

[16]Adapted from a booklet by Albrecht, K., *Total Quality Service* (Chicago: Leventhol & Horwath, 1988), p. 7.

[17]Ibid.

[18]Murphy, J. M. and Taylor, J. A., "Taking Quality as Seriously as Profits," *Industrial Engineering* 27, 1, January 1995, p. 28.

[19]Leibfried, K. J. J. and McNair, C. J., *Benchmarking* (New York: HarperCollins Publishing, 1992), p. 331.

[20] Zemke, R. "Peer Coaching: How to Manage When Managers Are Few and Far Between," *The Service Edge*, July 1996, p.6. Reprinted with permission of Lakewood Publications.

Winning Telephone Techniques
Making the most of your phone to boost customer satisfaction and loyalty[1]

The telephone is the cornerstone of any organization's general strategy and a crucial key to producing great customer service.

THE WAY IT IS . . .THE FRUSTRATIONS OF CARELESS TELEPHONE USE

The telephone certainly can be, as the ads used to say, "The next best thing to being there." In fact, no business can long survive without a phone. But there are two significant drawbacks to the telephone which can almost cancel out its benefits:

1. *Many people have never learned the basics of telephone courtesy and effectiveness.* They've been using the phone since childhood and have never polished their business telephone techniques. What may be everyday casual telephone usage at home may be totally inappropriate for business. The result can be customer dissatisfaction and a severe loss of organizational image and effectiveness.
2. *You cannot see the person you are talking with.* Thus, the phone does not permit most nonverbal communication. Without nonverbal cues to reinforce or clarify a message, the listener on the other end of the line may be easily mislead or confused.

Phrased another way, each telephone call creates interactions where people are operating blind—without the visual feedback that helps assign meaning to spoken messages.

To compensate for this lack of vision, we as callers create our own conclusions solely from auditory input. What we hear (or do not hear) conveys subtle messages through timing, tone of voice, word choice, and interruptions. For many people, this ambiguity makes telephone use uncomfortable and even threatening. Although it is a great piece of technology, the telephone can also be frustrating.

Here is a story about one incident where a company lost a customer because it forgot (or never stopped to think about) the drawbacks to telephone communication:

Garth enjoys working on old cars. A few years ago as he drove to work, he noticed a sports car in an auto dealership's lot. Sensing that such a car would do a lot for his image, Garth decided to inquire about it. He telephoned the dealership and here is how the conversation went.

A receptionist briskly identified the name of the dealership and, just as quickly, commanded, "Hold a minute, please." Fifteen seconds later the receptionist came back on the line and asked, "Can I help ya?" Garth asked to "speak to someone in used cars, please."

"Just a minute," the receptionist replied.

After a pause, a man's voice said, "Hello?"

"I'd like a little information about the Triumph TR-6 you have on your lot," Garth said.

"Ya mean the red one?"

"Yes. Could you give me some information on that car?"

The male voice hesitated for a moment and said, "I think that's the owner's daughter's car. She's been driving it around. Let me check and see what the deal is on it."

There was a long pause and while Garth waited on hold, another male voice came on the line saying, "Hello? Hello?" to which he replied, "I'm already being helped." There was a click as the interrupter hung up without acknowledging Garth's comment.

After a few more minutes, the original salesman came back on the line and said, "Yeah, I think that's the car the boss's daughter has been driving around. If they sell it, they'll want an arm and a leg for it. I think it's a '75 model."

"Well would you check and let me know if it's for sale?" Garth asked again, getting exasperated.

"Just a minute, I'll ask the owner," he said as he put Garth on hold again. After a few moments, the salesperson again picked up the telephone and abruptly said, "The owner says it's not for sale."

As Garth began to say, "Thanks for the information," he was cut off in midsentence by the click of the telephone as the man hung up.

Although this sales representative was probably not being intentionally rude, he sure came across that way. Garth was irritated to the point where he would definitely not do business with this dealership.

-------------------- *Learning Objectives* --------------------

After you have studied this chapter, you should be able to

1. Better understand your own attitudes toward telephone courtesy.

2. Recognize the kinds of telephone mannerisms that can lead to customer dissatisfaction.

3. Apply more than 20 techniques to improve your overall telephone effectiveness.

ACTION TIPS FOR TELEPHONE COURTESY

As we saw in our opening example, behaviors that come across as discourteous can quickly sour a caller's impression of a company. The remainder of this chapter offers specific tips for improving telephone courtesy and effectiveness.

ACTION TIP 1: CHECK YOUR PHONE USE ATTITUDES

The telephone is a powerful tool for sales, information gathering, and relationship building. By receiving and initiating calls, we can accomplish a lot. Yet some people are phone shy. They are hesitant to call others and sometimes hesitant about answering incoming calls.

Your attitudes can impact your telephone effectiveness.

Check your telephone-use attitudes using the self-evaluation below. It can help you understand some of your attitudes toward using the telephone. It can also help you improve your telephone techniques by showing what you may be doing wrong.

Circle the appropriate letter for each item: N = Never, SL = Seldom, SM = Sometimes, O = Often, A = Always. Then read the instructions at the end of the form.

How Often Do You . . .

Improvement Goal

1. Delay calling someone or fail to return a call?   N SL SM O A

2. Answer the telephone with a curt or mechanical greeting?   N SL SM O A

3. Let the phone ring, hoping the caller will give up?   N SL SM O A

4. Save travel time by calling   A O SM SL N
   for information ("let your
   fingers do the walking")?

5. End the conversation by   A O SM SL N
   summarizing what was
   agreed upon?

6. Solicit feedback about your   A O SM SL N
   customer service by phone call?

7. Put people on hold for   N SL SM O A
   more than a few seconds?

8. Have someone else place   N SL SM O A
   your calls for you?

9. Smile as you speak?   A O SM SL N

10. Speak clearly and in   A O SM SL N
    pleasant, conversational
    tones (no "stage voice")?

If you circled a letter in the two right columns for any of the items, your telephone techniques can use improvement. In the space provided to the right of these items, set specific goals for improvement in each area needed.

ACTION TIP 2: GIVE YOUR OWN COMPANY A CALL

A telephone call is often the first contact that a person has with an organization, and as the old saying goes, you never get a second chance to make a first impression. Callers draw many conclusions from the impressions received from a phone conversation. They create impressions about the person's and company's

- efficiency
- communication skills
- friendliness
- expertise

all in the first few moments of a telephone call. Recognize that a phone call is often the first point of contact a person has with you and your company. It's "where the rubber meets the road." In short, your courtesy and effectiveness quickly convey unspoken but important messages to calling customers.

Many customers get their first impression of you and your company from a phone call.

Managers should check on the telephone skills of their organization regularly. They should have someone who knows how the phones should be handled call periodically and then prepare a brief report.

ACTION TIP 3: ANSWER PROMPTLY

An answer after two rings or less conveys efficiency and a willingness to serve. When the telephone rings longer, callers get the feeling that you are unavailable and that their call is an intrusion. What is worse is that unanswered callers get the message that you think they are not important.

ACTION TIP 4: BE PREPARED TO HANDLE CALLS

Be sure that your work area is set up for comfortable and efficient telephone use. Place the telephone at a comfortable spot on your desk or worktable. Keep your frequently called numbers list current and have material you may need to refer to within reach.

Have note paper, message slips and pens handy. Use a planner system or desk calendar that has room to jot down notes about conversations you have. Get the caller's name and number as soon as possible and summarize the conversations briefly—especially any commitments you will need to follow up.

> Always have note-taking materails handy by the phone.

If you agree to do something for a caller, be sure to write it down and then check it off when completed.

ACTION TIP 5: PLACE YOUR OWN CALLS

Some business people think it is a sign of status to have their secretary place telephone calls for them. But when most people have someone else place a call for them, it comes across as impersonal or even arrogant. It seems to set them up as seeing themselves as more important than the person they are calling.

ACTION TIP 6: AVOID UNNECESSARY CALL SCREENING

Each person should also be encouraged to answer his or her own telephone unless they are busy in a face-to-face conversation with a customer. Routine screening of calls by a secretary or receptionist often creates resentment in the caller. The constant use of "May I say who is calling?" is recognized as a dodge—an opportunity for the person to decide if he or she wants to talk or not.

The appropriate way to answer a business call is to simply state your name or your department and your name. Example: "Customer support. This is Nancy Chin." Calling yourself Mrs., Ms., Mr., or a title may sound a bit self-important. Example: "Accounting office, Mr. Silvia speaking." Some people use just their last name, although this can sometimes con-

> As a caller, use good business etiquette by identifying yourself immediately.

fuse callers. (A manager friend named Paul Waite found his last-name-only greeting often followed by a very long pause!)

Use of "How may I help you?" (Or a similar phrase) following your name tells your caller whom they are speaking to, and that you are ready to converse with them. When answering another person's telephone, be sure to identify both that other person and yourself. Example: "Michelle Theron's office. This is Shelly Sampson. May I help you?"

Of course, receptionists would never need to ask who is calling if *callers* would use good business etiquette. Good manners dictate that when we call people, we identify ourselves immediately. Example: "Good morning, Barry Adamson calling. Is Sharon Silverstein there?" Get in the habit of doing this and you will set a good example for others who may realize the advantage of such courtesy.

ACTION TIP 7: USE COURTESY TITLES

While calling yourself Mr. or Ms. may sound stuffy, don't assume that a caller prefers to be called by his or her first name. Use proper titles for the people to whom you refer. If in doubt whether to use a first name, call the person by the more formal "Mr." or "Ms." If they prefer the more informal first name, they will say so. It is better to be a little too formal than overly familiar.

Titles and formality can create credibility. If you refer to other professionals, refer to them formally. You'd be a bit thrown off if a medical doctor introduced himself: "Hi, I'm Larry, your brain surgeon." Even if your organization has an informal culture, don't assume that others do.

ACTION TIP 8: THANK PEOPLE FOR CALLING OR RECEIVING YOUR CALL

"Thank you" is the most powerful phrase in human relations. Express appreciation regularly. Some companies use it as a greeting: "Thank you for calling Avis." A "thanks for calling" at the end of a conversation is also a strong customer satisfaction booster. It reassures the customer that you are interested in serving and that their call was not an intrusion.

ACTION TIP 9: KEEP YOUR CONVERSATION TACTFUL AND BUSINESSLIKE

Nothing turns off a customer or caller like poor wording. I've had experiences where upon telling people my name they say, "Who?" rather abruptly. Few things make a caller feel less appreciated. If you didn't catch the name, ask politely: "I'm sorry, I didn't get your name, sir. Would you repeat it?"

Keep your comments positive and oriented toward solving the caller's problem or concern. Don't just toss the ball back when you can't immediately help. Don't say anything that makes people or your organization look unprofessional or uncaring.

Here are some other dos and don'ts:

Don't Say	Do Say
Who is this?	May I ask who's calling?
What's your name?	I'm sorry, but I didn't get your name.
What do you need?	How can I help you?
Speak up please.	I'm sorry, I can't hear you. Could you speak a little louder?
Well, I wasn't the one you talked to.	I'm sorry, Ms. James, someone else must have talked to you, but I'll be happy to help.
He's out to lunch.	Mr. Barringer is away from the office for about one hour. Can I ask him to call you back?
You'll need to call our billing office.	That information is available in our billing office. I'll be happy to connect you. (Or, shall I ask someone in billing to call you back?)
Sorry, I can't help you with that.	I don't have that information here. May I have someone from our quality service department give you a call?
There's nothing I can do about that.	I'll put that on my calendar for next Tuesday and I'll check on your request again. Then I'll call you back.

ACTION TIP 10: SPEAK CLEARLY AND DISTINCTLY

Hold the telephone mouthpiece about a half inch from your lips. Whether you answer with your name, the company name, or the department name, speak clearly and distinctly. Example: Carefully say "Good morning, Primo Computer Service," "Hello, this is KJQQ radio," or "Scheduling Department," followed by your name. Separate the words with tiny pauses.

Don't answer with just the abbreviations of your organization. I recently called Piedmont Community College and was greeted with just an abrupt, "P-C-C." I wasn't sure what was being said and the receptionist lost an opportunity to set a better first impression.

> Make your telephone greeting informative, friendly, and sincere.

Even if you say these words a hundred times a day, resist the temptation to get lazy or to repeat the greeting in a mechanical, unfriendly manner. Remember that each caller hears your greeting just once, even though you have said it many times. Make it fresh and sincere.

ACTION TIP 11: SPEAK NATURALLY AND COMFORTABLY

Talk to your caller as you would to a friend. Use warm, friendly voice tones and natural spontaneous reactions. If a caller says something humorous, laugh. If his or her tone of voice suggests tension or even anger, it may be appropriate to comment on that: "You sound upset, is there something I can do to help."

A strong, clear voice is a tremendous asset. It conveys confidence and high credibility. But even if a person is not gifted with the voice of a professional broadcaster, he or she can do things with the voice that creates and holds listener interest.

The key to holding interest is *variation* in the voice. People cannot pay attention to something that does not change. But we do perk up when speakers adjust their voice. The three things any speaker can vary are pitch, loudness, and rate.

Pitch is almost a musical quality: the place on a musical scale where the voice would be. Male speakers tend to have more trouble varying pitch than females. The problem, of course, is that too little variation in pitch sounds like a monotone. In a word, it is boring.

Another problem is that people try to force their voice into a different pitch. By artificially speaking too low or too high, we create a stage voice that sounds phony. Use your natural range, but experiment with broadening that range too.

Some speakers do not want to risk much variation. They fear sound-

> By working on vocal variety, you can improve your ability to convey a range of feelings.

ing silly. Failing to vary pitch is like throwing away one of your most useful tools for effective communication. Listen carefully to good radio or TV announcers, comedians, or other entertainers. You will find that they vary their pitch a lot. Try pushing your range of pitch outward a bit. Go a little higher and a little lower than you typically do and you will find listeners more interested in what you have to say.

ACTION TIP 12: DO NOT LET "DEAD AIR" HAPPEN

Broadcasters call those awkward gaps when nothing is being broadcast "dead air." Listeners have no idea what is going on and often change stations if the silence persists. The same can happen with a telephone call.

If you need to transfer a caller, look up some information, or read some material, *tell the caller what you are doing.* Remember, he or she cannot see you. Use statements such as these to reassure your caller that you are still with him or her:

> "I will transfer you to Mr. Kovak now. He can get you that information. One moment please."
> "I understand your concern. Ms. Jessop in our billing department can best help you with that. May I put you on hold for a moment? I will see if she is in."
> "I'm reviewing your account now, Mr. Jenson. Let me just check a few figures and I can give you that information in a moment."

Putting people on hold can be annoying to callers, but you can reduce this annoyance by telling them what you are doing and why.

Always acknowledge comments audibly. Be sure to react to your caller's conversation. Since your callers can't see you and don't receive visual feedback from you, they must rely on your spoken feedback—on what you say—to determine whether you understand what is being said.

By frequently saying "yes" or "I see" or "uh-huh" or "I agree" you are providing the needed feedback. Don't let caller comments go unacknowledged. Stamp out dead air.

ACTION TIP 13: TAKE MESSAGES CHEERFULLY AND ACCURATELY

Be willing to take messages for others. Keep a note pad handy to record key words and phrases. Read the message back to the caller to be sure it is accurate. Then be sure to pass the message to the right person. Most organizations use message forms such as the one illustrated. Fill out the form completely and legibly.

As you write a message slip, be complete. To avoid possible communication problems, it is especially important to:

1. *Get the full name and correct spelling.* If you don't understand it clearly, ask the caller to spell it for you. Let him know why you are asking for the spelling by saying something like, "I want to make sure the message is accurate. Will you spell your name?"
2. *Ask for the name of the organization if appropriate.* The best reason for this is that it may give the message receiver a hint as to the nature of the call. It can also be a way of double-checking if there is a mistake with the number.

To_____	☐ URGENT	
Date _____Time _____	A.M. P.M.	

WHILE YOU WERE OUT

From _____

of _____

Phone _____
Area Code   Number   Extension

Telephoned		Please call	
Came to see you		Wants to see you	
Returned your call		Will call again	

Message _____

_____

_____

_____

_____

_____

_____

Signed _____

Fill out telephone message slips fully so the receiver
will be ready to return the call.

3. *Get the full telephone number, including the area code if it's long distance.* If the caller says, "She has it," you can say politely, "I know she can get back to you even faster if I jot your number down with your message."
4. If the caller doesn't volunteer any specific message, it will save on the callback if you ask, *"Is there any information you would like to leave that may be helpful to Ms. Jones when she calls you back?"*
5. *Say, "Thank you," and tell the caller that you will give the person the message as soon as he or she is available.* Say this with assurance.
6. *Note the time and date the message was taken, and add your initials in case there are any questions.*

ACTION TIP 14: SMILE

Picture the person you are talking with and treat her as though you were face-to-face with a friend. Be pleasant. Be concerned. Be helpful. Physically smiling somehow comes through the telephone line via your voice tones.

Keep a mirror by the telephone to remind yourself to smile. It really does come through to the caller.

ACTION TIP 15: TO END A CONVERSATION, STAND UP

Like smiling, the behavior of standing somehow conveys to your caller that you are finished—just as it would to someone talking to you in person. This works particularly well if the social chitchat seems to be going on too long. Most callers will take the hint.

ACTION TIP 16: BE SURE THE CONVERSATION IS FINISHED BEFORE YOU HANG UP

If you initiated the call, take the responsibility for ending it. Use conclusion words such as "Thank you for your help" or "That is just what I needed."

If you received the call, be sure the caller is finished. In our opening story, Garth was about to ask the salesperson if the dealership had any other sports cars available, but was cut off before he could.

Many people have telephone answering machines or voice mail. Both are convenient for capturing otherwise lost messages. Answering machines save messages on cassette tapes or in digital memory; voice mail is a computer message center. In both cases, callers are invited to leave a message when you are not available. If you use an answering machine or voice mail, try these ideas.

ACTION TIP 17: MAKE YOUR GREETING MESSAGE EFFICIENT

When you are not available, callers do not want to listen to a long or clever message. Record your message to be brief. Messages like the following usually work fine:

> "You have reached 555-1131. We cannot take your call now. Please leave a message at the tone." (Note: This message does not identify who you are and may provide privacy and security.)
>
> "This is Acme Manufacturing's Warehouse. Our business hours are from 8 a.m. to 6 p.m. Monday through Friday. Please leave a message at the tone."
>
> "Thank you for calling NuHousing, Inc.—your mobile home leader. Please leave a message at the tone and we will get back to you as soon as we can. Thank you."

Recorded messages may also ask for specific information from callers ("If you have your account number available, please leave it so we can respond to your request more quickly"). Do not, however, ask for too much. Also, assure the caller that you will return the call.

> Keep your message brief and concise. Callers know what to do.

When you leave a message on another person's machine, be sure to state the following:

- Your name (spoken clearly and spelled if necessary)
- Time and day of your call
- A brief explanation of why you are calling
- Your phone number
- When you can be reached.

Here are two examples:

> "This is Jim Steadman calling. It's 7 PM Friday. I have a question about your new Wave Runners. Please call me at 555-3077 after 10 AM Saturday."
>
> "This is Raul Sanchez—that is spelled S-A-N-C-H-E-Z. I am inter-

ested in your job opening for an experienced night programmer and would like to arrange an interview. I have six years experience with a company like yours. Please call me at 555-0819 after 6 PM today, Thursday the 4th. Thank you."

Some answering machines can be annoying.
By permission of Johnny Hart and Creators Syndicate, Inc.

ACTION TIP 18: LEARN TO USE YOUR PHONE'S FEATURES

The wonderful world of telephone technology is constantly coming up with new features. Unfortunately, like the 80 percent of people who have no idea how to program a VCR, many business people haven't learned to use the many tricks available through their phone system.

A recent study of IBM customer complaints found that customer dissatisfaction with the firm's phone-call handling stemmed from two general classes:

1. The inability of employees to use the features of telephone and voice mail systems, and
2. Shortcomings in treating customers with the highest degree of courtesy.

IBM responded to these concerns by providing additional training for all employees. Such training boosted customer satisfaction with the firm's telephone responsiveness dramatically.[2]

If you are uncertain about the use of your telephone system's features, call the company. They will be happy to have a representative teach you how to use the system. After all, it is in their best interest to have you using the equipment fully—so that they have a satisfied customer.

ACTION TIP 19: CONSIDER USING A HEADSET PHONE

If you spend a sizable percentage of your day on the phone, consider getting a headset rather than having to hold the receiver to your ear. Likewise, if you find that you frequently have to step away from the phone for information while the caller holds, consider using a cordless phone that allows you to continue talking while you move about.

> A headset phone is very convenient for people who are on the phone a lot.

Telephone and electronics stores have a wide variety of headsets and portable telephones to choose from.

ACTION TIP 20: USE THE HOLD BUTTON CAREFULLY

What may seem to you like a brief hold, can seem awfully long to a caller. Even if your phone system plays music, callers get pretty upset after 30 seconds or so. Try timing the next time you are put on hold. A minute can seem like an eternity.

Use a portable cordless phone to keep voice contact or pick up every 15 to 20 seconds to let the caller know that you haven't forgotten him or her.

If you anticipate a fairly long hold time, offer to call back or at least prepare the caller by saying that this will require several minutes to complete. Then give him the option of holding or awaiting a callback.

The telephone can be a time waster as well as a time saver. Since many of us spend a sizable amount of our business time on the phone, it is important to be as efficient as possible. Here are some further tips that will help.

ACTION TIP 21: PLAN YOUR CALLS FOR EFFICIENCY

Although small talk is sometimes useful to create a good relationship with callers, strive to make business calls concise without being curt, or abrupt. This can be especially important when using portable cellular telephones because both the receiver of the call and the caller are billed for "air time"—the time you use the cellular network. Even for local calls, charges can run 50 cents per minute or more, depending on the time of day.

When placing a business call, plan what you will say, preferably in writing. Jot down some notes that include:

1. The purpose of your call, and
2. A list of information you need to get or give.

Be sure to identify yourself and the reason for your call early in the conversation. Business people do not like playing "guess who?" or "guess what?" A good way to kick off a typical call would be to say:

"Hello. This is Tina Watson calling from Unicorn Corporation. Is Marilyn Smith in?"

Once connected with Ms. Smith, say:

"Hello Ms. Smith. This is Tina Watson with Unicorn Corporation. I need to get some information about your recent catalog order. Is this a good time for you to talk?"

Notice that the caller here identifies herself, previews what she needs to discuss, and also asks about the person's readiness to talk. If the person is busy and cannot give your call full attention, this gives them a chance to offer to call you back.

> Prepare for your calls in advance to maximize efficiency.

When you need to return calls to people who have called you, schedule them at times they are likely to be in. Be aware of probable lunch hours and long-distance time differences. If you do not, you are likely to play that dreaded game: telephone tag. You keep returning calls and just missing the person who is trying to call you.

ACTION TIP 22: TIME CALLBACKS FOR EFFICIENCY

Be specific about when you plan to call a person back. Vague statements like "I'll get back to you on that" may create unrealistic expectations. The caller expects to hear from you within 15 minutes while you meant 2 or 3 hours.

Instead say, "I can call you back between 1 and 2 this afternoon" and, of course, *do it during that time frame.*

Avoid business callbacks during typical lunch time or at times other than normal business hours. Some people intentionally call when they expect that the person will not be there—especially if they don't really want to talk anyhow. Leaving a message allows them to toss the ball back to the original caller, but it too often results in an extended game of telephone tag. That wastes time.

ACTION TIP 23: DON'T LET THE TELEPHONE INTERRUPT AN IMPORTANT LIVE CONVERSATION

One of the pet peeves of many customers is when their discussion with a business person is interrupted by a phone call. If you are talking live to someone, do not assume that the phone call is more important or should be accorded priority.

> "Live," face-to-face customers almost always take precedence over phone calls.

If you must take the call, always excuse yourself and, when you determine what the call is about, inform the caller that you have someone with you now and will be happy to call them back in a specified time.

ACTION TIP 24: KEEP CALLERS ON TRACK

If a caller digresses into chitchat or nonessential conversation, use a bridging technique to get back on track. This often calls for some creativity, but give it a try.

If your caller says:

"I get really sick of this gloomy weather around here. It really gets to you after a while, don't you think?"

You might say:

Well, one way we can brighten your day is to . . . get this billing problem straightened out. . . [or] get that new recliner ordered for you . . . [or] give you the information you've been wanting.

If your caller says:

"How about those Buffalo Bill's last week. They never looked tougher. Kelly is still the best QB in the league, don't you think?"

You might say:

"They were good. I hope I can get your *bill*s straightened out for you real soon . . . [or] which reminds me, we need to be looking long and deep into your financial plan. . . [or] let's tackle this order for you."

If your caller says:

I really appreciate your help with the Special Olympics last week-end. Your company is a big help.

You might say:

Well thank you, Ms. Knowaki. I hope I can help you find that widgit you called about too. Let's see. Here it is . . .

If your caller wants to chat on and on, take charge: "Mrs. Customer, let me summarize what you've said and then if there is anything else you need to tell me, you can fill in."

If your caller is exceptionally upset, let them get it all out before you attempt to interrupt. An interruption will just make them angrier. As they describe their anger, offer sympathetic comments that let them know that you are still listening: "I see" or "Wow, that doesn't sound like we treated you very well," or "I know how upsetting that can be."

ACTION TIP 25: HANDLE THE UPSET CALLER WITH TACT AND SKILL

Here are some additional tips for dealing with upset callers. First, recognize that there are two phases to handling upset or difficult people:

Step One: Understand Why They Are Upset or Difficult

The three common root causes of anger/frustration arise from peoples' feelings that:

1. They are not valued or important
2. They are helpless
3. "It" just isn't fair.

We have all experienced these feelings at some time. Be empathic and recognize that these don't make the caller a bad person but rather a person who is having an unpleasant experience. Try to put yourself in their position. Then,

Step Two: Diffuse the Anger or Frustration with Statements or Questions Like:

1. *Help me to understand* . This will encourage them to explain why they are upset. Don't try to defend or argue with their perceptions—

they know what they feel, even if it doesn't make a lot of sense to you. Then, let them know that you empathize by saying,

2. *I can understand why you would feel that way.* Do not say "I know *exactly* what you mean" because you probably don't. Instead convey that you have an idea of what he or she might be feeling. Then ask,

3. *What would be a good solution from your point of view?* This begins to shift the conversation away from the venting of emotion toward solution seeking.

Strive to have the caller share the responsibility for finding a reasonable solution to the problem being experienced. When he has made a proposal or suggested an idea that might work, you can begin a negotiating process that can lead to a reconciliation—and to a cooling off of the caller.

ACTION TIP 26: BRING THE CONVERSATION TO A PLEASANT BUT EFFICIENT CLOSE

It can be tempting to talk on with friendly people, but others may be waiting to talk to you and other work awaits. Try some of these techniques for tactfully closing a conversation even when the caller seems to want to go on:

1. Summarize the call and what has been decided. Say, "Let me go over what we decided to do" or "Let me summarize the process for you." Spell out what has been done: "I closed that account and transferred $1000 to your new fund." "That is all you need to do for now. It has been taken care of."

2. Speak in the past tense. "As we discussed" or "That was all the information I needed" or "I'm glad that you called."

3. Say "thank you for calling." This is a universal clue that the conversation is over.

4. End the call positively by saying, "I've enjoyed talking with you, Mr. Blanko."

ACTION TIP 27: ALWAYS RETURN YOUR OWN PHONE CALLS

Although it is not always pleasant, it is necessary to return calls unless you have an exceptionally good reason. If you don't, you're offending the person who called you and will risk getting a reputation as one who ignores people who call.

If people call who are trying to sell you something you can't use, return their call and deal assertively with them. Tell them pleasantly but directly, that you don't want to do business. By ignoring their calls, you

Failure to return a phone call conveys arrogance or lack of caring about the caller.

show a disregard for their time and effort. Do them a favor and simply say no.

ACTION TIP 28: PLAN YOUR OUTGOING CALLS CAREFULLY

Few things are as embarrassing as getting someone on the line and then forgetting why you called. Take a few moments before calling to jot down the questions or information you need to share. Then check them off as you speak.

ACTION TIP 29: CALL BACK IF YOU ARE DISCONNECTED

The person who originated the call is responsible for re-establishing contact if the line is interrupted.

ACTION TIP 30: ALWAYS ASK: "IS THIS A CONVENIENT TIME TO TALK"

Too many callers burst into their message when the person being called may be involved in something else. If there is any possibility that the person may be busy, ask if this is a good time before you begin.

Get into the habit of asking if this is a convenient time to talk.

If asked that question and it really isn't a good time, let the caller know and arrange another time to talk that would be more convenient.

This tip also holds if you don't have information you may need to answer a caller's questions. Be honest and tell him so. Then arrange a call-back.

ACTION TIP 31: CONSISTENTLY WORK TO IMPROVE YOUR TELEPHONE SKILLS

Good telephone skills are essential for career success in almost every field. Make it an ongoing effort to get feedback about your skill level. Take the opportunity to attend seminars or view training videos that teach new and specialized skills.

If you supervise other people, don't hesitate to critique their telephone skills. Be frank with them if some things they are doing are inconsistent with the tips in this book. Remind them of the critical importance—to the company and to their professionalism—of good telephone skills.

Be observant. Listen carefully to both the spoken and unspoken messages that may be sent to your callers.

Remember that when you use the telephone, your communication channel is limited. There are no visual cues being sent—your callers can't see you. So help them "see" you in the best possible light by your use of winning telephone techniques.

A FINAL THOUGHT . . .

The telephone is a powerful tool for customer service when used correctly. Often a phone call is the customer's first or only contact with your organization. Using proper telephone techniques is critical to setting and maintaining good impressions and effective communication. Applying the tips described above will put you way ahead of most organizations in your phone use.

------------------- *Summary of Key Ideas* -------------------

▶ Careless or ineffective telephone use can be a major turnoff to potential customers.

▶ A variety of usage tips are presented for better phone-call handling, both incoming and outgoing. People who use these tips will greatly improve the likelihood of meeting or exceeding customer expectations, thus creating customer loyalty.

Application Activity 1
Identify the Errors in Garth's Call

Reread this story of Garth's call to the car dealership at the beginning of this chapter. Then describe four or more telephone use problems that probably lead to Garth's irritation and his decision not to do business with that dealer.

Problem 1:

Problem 2:

Problem 3:

Problem 4:

Most people who hear of this incident quickly identify the unspoken message projected loud and clear by the dealership: This caller (and potential customer) isn't particularly important. Perhaps this is because the car in question isn't for sale (and the short-sighted salesperson can't see any advantage to be gained by being polite) or, perhaps it is because their telephone usage is hopelessly rude and unprofessional. They've forgotten or have never learned the basics of telephone courtesy.

Whatever the reason, the outcome is the same: a caller who has been treated poorly and will harbor some resentment against this business.

Clearly, poor telephone techniques can have a dramatic impact on a company's success. Winning telephone techniques build stronger relationships with customers and other people important to the organization. And employees who master such techniques are particularly valuable to the company.

Application Activity 2

Try Rewording for a Better Tone

See if you can rephrase the following statements to make the wording positive and tactful. Also strive to solve the caller's concern as efficiently as possible:

1. Bill is out playing golf again. I doubt that he'll be back in the office today.

2. Sarah went to the restroom and then is going to lunch for about an hour or so.

3. Who did you say you were?

4. You say you've been trying to get through? When did you try?

5. Who are you holding for?

6. This is Bobby. What do you need?

7. Hey, sorry about that. I got backed up and couldn't call you back.

8. We don't do that kind of work here.

9. Try again after five, okay?

10. Sally used to work here but we let her go. Maybe I can help.

Application Activity 3
Hear the Difference

Try this simple exercise to demonstrate how voice inflection can change the meaning of what you say. Repeat out loud the following sentence, first just using your normal voice.

"Henry didn't show up for work today."

Now restate the same sentence with surprise in your voice.
Next, make it sound like a secret.
Finally, turn it into a question.

Next, try saying the following sentence with the emphasis on a different word each time:

"I think Doris can do that."

Notice that when you emphasize the word "I," the unspoken message may be "I think she can do it, although maybe no one else thinks so." When you emphasize the word "think" it conveys an unspoken message of uncertainty.

Listen for the possible unspoken messages as you emphasized "Doris," "can," and "that." Notice how these subtle changes in voice and emphasis can convey widely different meanings.

Application Activity 4
Critique this Call

The following situation describes a fairly commonplace business telephone conversation. In the space provided at the right, critique what is going on. Note both effective and ineffective techniques used by each speaker.

The Story   *My Critique*

Diane: Good morning, marketing department. This is Diane. May I help you?

Bobbi: Hi, is this marketing? Oh good. I need to find out some information about your future seminar schedule. Let me see now. . .[pause] there are several cities where our people might want to attend. [pause] I've got a list here some-where. I know Cleveland is one. . .

Diane: We do have seminars scheduled for Cleveland, but which programs are you interested in?

Bobbi: I'm not real sure. My boss just asked me to get a schedule from you. Don't you have a secretary training class?

Diane: Yes. In fact we have three profes-sional secretaries' programs. One is for the new employee and the others for advanced—those with two years' expe-rience or more—and one that focuses on word processing.

Bobbi: Oh, good. Oh, here it is. I found my list of cities. The Cleveland, Buffalo, Denver, and Biloxi offices all seem interested. They said they saw a brochure about your company.

Diane: Do you have one of our brochures?

Bobbi: No, I haven't seen it.

Diane: Okay. Here's what I think we should do. I will send you a brochure with the list of cities and dates for our seminars. Let's see. We will be in Cleve-land, Buffalo, and Denver in the next two months, but not Biloxi. Perhaps there is a nearby city your Biloxi people could go to. I'll send you a complete list and you can handle the registration by phone or FAX. Will this be satisfactory?

Bobbi: Great. Sounds perfect. You will include pricing and everything, I assume?

Diane: I sure will. And I know your people will love the seminars. They're really neat. Now, can I get your name and address? I'll get this information into the mail today. . .

Reviewing the Case

1. What was accomplished by Diane's greeting?

2. What did Bobbi fail to do in her opening remarks?

3. What information did Bobbi need to make this a successful conversation?

4. How well did Diane handle the call?

5. What would you do differently if you were Bobbi? If you were Diane?

6. Did you notice the ways Diane reassured the customer? Why is that important?

7. How was the overall efficiency of this call?

Application Activity 5

Getting Back on Track

See if you can tactfully get the conversation back on track when your caller digresses. Write a bridging comment that might help you do so:

1. My daughter is getting married on November 19 so things have been pretty hectic here at home.

2. With all the playoff excitement, I haven't been able to concentrate on getting this accounting problem taken care of. Can you believe that comeback in last night's game?

3. The kids are growing too fast. Just yesterday my youngest asked for a new guitar so he can join a rock band. He's only 13.

4. That reminds me of the time I made my first birdie playing golf. It was a cool but clear day and I was playing pretty lousy until the 13th hole—lucky 13.

NOTES

[1]Material in this chapter is adapted from a videotape training program and book, *Winning Telephone Tips,* © 1994, Paul R. Timm, Inc., 81 E. 2000 South, Orem Utah, 84058 and Jack Wilson and Associates, Inc., 411 S. Sangamon Street, Chicago, IL 60612. All rights reserved. Reproducing any part of this publication without written permission of the author and publisher is prohibited (except where noted).

[2] Estabrooke, M. and Foy, N. F., "Answering the Call of Tailored Training," in *Training,* October 1992, p.85.

Writing for Customer Service
Using written messages to boost customer satisfaction and loyalty[1]

Some people would rather eat a bar of soap than write a business letter.

THE WAY IT IS . . . FOLLOW-UP NOTES ARE GOOD BUSINESS[2]

When I was a manager trainee in my first job out of college, I sent a letter to the college recruiter who had hired me. The letter was brief—it simply said how much I enjoyed working for the company and how he had helped me. I received a call from him a few days later. He thanked me for the letter and commented that of all the trainees he had worked with, I was the only one who had written to him in this way.

Interestingly, a short while later he was instrumental in my getting promoted to a better position.

Best-selling author, Harvey Mackay talks about "short notes [that] yield long results" in his book *Swim with the Sharks without Being Eaten Alive*. He comments on how few people send follow-up notes to customers, even those who have made a major purchase, like a car. Another glaring omission of many people interviewing for a job is the follow-up thank you note to the interviewer.

Mackay cites many successful people who constantly send out short but effective notes with messages like "I want you to know how much I enjoyed our meeting/interview/your gift/your hospitality" or "Congratulations on your new house/car/tennis trophy."

The moral of the story: Don't hesitate to let people know that you appreciate them, and *do it in writing*. Don't worry too much about formality or business letter protocol. Often a handwritten note, written conversationally, works fine. Just do it.

-------------------- *Learning Objectives* --------------------

After you have studied this chapter, you should be able to

1. Recognize the value of thank you notes, especially when the customer doesn't expect one.

2. Apply the most important tips on goodwill messages: Just do it and be original.

3. Apply four tips to enhance the power of appreciation messages.

4. Use news releases to generate interest in your organization and attract potential customers.

Thank you letters are often sent by businesses that sell high price items like cars, trucks, appliances, furniture, and the like. But companies are increasingly recognizing the value of the thank you note to buyers of even lower-priced items. I recently received a note of appreciation from the owner of the athletic shoe store where I'd just purchased some jogging shoes.

Why do this? Because such correspondence can form the beginning of an ongoing business relationship. It tells the customer that he or she is important to you and that you are available to serve further. Written notes to customers are an often overlooked way to create that all important one-to-one relationship. In this chapter we will consider the power of such letters which are called goodwill messages.

SOME TIPS ON USING GOODWILL MESSAGES

A goodwill note or letter is one you write even though you don't have to. Many people, by failing to send goodwill messages, overlook an excellent opportunity to promote good feelings toward and within their organization. Applying the power of written communication can quickly set one organization apart from most others. So the first tip is

Just Do It

Few things make an employee—an internal customer—feel better than to receive a brief letter of appreciation, congratulations, sympathy, or concern from the boss or a coworker. It only takes the writer a minute, yet it can help to develop good employee relations. Likewise, customers who receive sincere, personal messages from people they do business with will likely harbor more favorable feelings toward that person and organization.

A manager friend of mine makes it a point to send short letters to the homes of employees whose work was exemplary. The payoff for such a simple action is that

1. The employee knows he recognizes and appreciates their good work;
2. By sending it home, he allows the employee's family to share in the praise;
3. The letter becomes a part of the employee's personnel file and can be used when preparing a performance review; and
4. By noting that copies have been sent to higher levels of management (cc: The boss) the employee knows he or she is getting additional attention.

Opportunities for goodwill notes come up almost daily. Besides on-the-job performance, personal and family accomplishments can be acknowledged. A daughter's wedding, an impressive bowling score, and recognition for community service can all be opportunities to show you care.

If you can't think of a reason to send a note to a customer or friend, perhaps you can clip a story or article out of a magazine that you know he or she is interested in. Send that with a brief note acknowledging that you are aware of their interest.

Be Original

A second tip on the use of goodwill messages is be original. At one time, sending Christmas cards was an effective way to plant your company's name before current and prospective customers. "People can't help feeling warmly about you," says John Kahl, president and CEO of Manco Inc., a "60-million marketer of a line of tapes, weather stripping, and mail supplies. But says Kahl, there is only so much warmth to go around. So many companies now send cards that yours can get lost in the shuffle. That's why he has added other, less popular holidays to his mailing roster: Thanksgiving, St. Patrick's Day, and the Fourth of July, to be specific. "It's a good way to break through," he claims.

To heighten interest, he has the cards designed in-house so they're different from run-of-the-mill cards. "People open them up just to see what the next one will look like," says Kahl, whose mailing list includes some 30,000 people. "It's a much more personal way to reach them."[3]

> Look for opportunities to send a variety of written messages to customers, internal and external. Few things will better set you apart from the many people and organizations who fail to do so.

A SALES FOLLOW-UP LETTER

The following letter is sent to customers who buy automobiles from a Chevy Dealer. As you'll see, it combines goodwill with some useful instructions.

Christensen
CHEVROLET / BUICK / GEO

Jan 6, 1995

Helen L. Timm
Paul R. Timm
81 E. 2000 st.
Orem UT 84058

Dear Paul and Helen:

We appreciate your business and the opportunity to work with you. Below is some information you will find helpful.

We normally receive your license plates about four weeks after all the paperwork from the sale is completed. We will send you a postcard when the plates are ready to be picked up here at our Cashier's window.

The title is issued by the state government and will be sent directly to the firm that loaned the money for the vehicle. If you paid cash, the title should reach you about two months following the completion of the paperwork from the sale.

Our Service and Parts Departments are open Monday through Friday for regular service. A courtesy bus is available at no charge in the Provo-Orem area Monday-Friday. Please call when your car needs servicing to make an appointment in order to minimize delays.

Chevrolet, Buick and Geo all send out important survey forms to a percentage of our customers during the first month after the sale and again at 5 months. We strive to make our customers *very satisfied.* If you are not, please let us know first. When you receive a survey form, please take the time to fill it out and return it in the envelope provided.

We care about you as our customer and look forward to a continued business relationship. Our goal is to be deserving of your future business.

Sincerely yours,

Mike Echevarria

Mike Echevarria

Marc Ensign

Marc Ensign
General Manager

A Look Inside
Critique the Letter

You can learn a lot from the examples of others. Get into the habit of critiquing business letters you receive. Create a list of your likes and dislikes. Start with the letter from the Chevy dealer above. List five likes and dislikes and then summarize what you'd do differently if you were to write such a letter.

Likes	Dislikes
1.	1.
2.	2.
3.	3.
4.	4.
5.	5.

How I'd improve this letter:

Please remember that there is no absolute, *right* way to create such a message. It's effectiveness ultimately depends upon the receiver's interpretation.

In this chapter we will consider the power of routine informative and goodwill messages. When you have finished this chapter you should be able to prepare effective one-to-one relationship-building messages with ease.

USE ROUTINE INFORMATIVE MESSAGES

Routine messages answer simple questions. Typical examples are letters that ask for or offer explanations or letters that order a product being advertised. The receiver of such a message is likely to be happy to get it. For the receiver, it answers questions and for the sender it presents an opportunity for relationship building.

> Routine informative messages answer simple questions or make easy requests.

Routine letters and memos are an essential part of business. For many companies they represent the bulk of business writing. Some common topics for routine writing include announcements, inquiries about products or services, letters granting a request, letters of introduction, etc.

An example of an announcement letter follows:

BRONSON SECURITY SYSTEMS
Keeping an Eye on Your Assets

Mr. Blaine Wilson, President
NuWay Technology
12777 Highway 50
Orlando, FL 27002

Dear Mr. Wilson:

    At Bronson Security Systems, we're always looking for better ways to serve your needs for plant security. I think we've found another in Arnold (Bucky) Corridini.

    Bucky has joined us as Coordinator of Surveillance Services. He will help us maintain and improve the high standard of quality service you've come to expect from Bronson.

    Of all the candidates we considered for this position, we found Bucky offered the best combination of ability, enthusiasm, and professionalism. Most important, he is the kind of person we want working on your account at NuWay Technology—the best!

    I'm confident you'll see this valuable addition to our staff as further evidence that we are committed to our clients. I've asked Bucky to personally introduce himself to you within the next week. If there's anything he or I can do for you, please call.

    Thank you for doing business with us.

Sincerely,

Guido Lambini, President
BRONSON SECURITY SYSTEMS

The samples above give you a feel for the types of written messages that can be used to build customer relationships. Think about how you might change their tone or content to better fit your personal communication style. Remember, just because these appear in print in a book does not mean they are perfect for all occasions and audiences. Your personal touch can dramatically improve these. Remember, communication is an art and you are the artist.

> Get into the habit of critiquing the letters you receive. Then develop your own style.

THREE GENERAL GUIDELINES FOR ROUTINE MESSAGES

Writers should apply the following principles when writing routine letters: Be direct, be complete, and be polite.

Be Direct

A writer can do little to destroy the effectiveness of a blatantly good-news message. The intent is to tell readers something they are glad to hear or, at worst, are neutral toward. People value efficiency of communication. Keep goodwill letters brief, although not curt—and to the point.

Service Snapshot

The Ultimate Electronics Difference

Bill decided to buy his compact disc player at Ultimate Electronics. He'd heard positive things about the store and decided to give it a try. He had this to say of the experience:

> I personally get very frustrated when I go into a store and I have to find someone to help me. Fortunately, I was attended to at Ultimate Electronics. I learned what I needed to about the different styles and then purchased the model that fit my needs. About a week later, I got a letter addressed to me with no return address. When I pulled out the small card inside the envelope and read it, I was pleasantly surprised. The Ultimate Electronic salesperson who helped me had sent a hand-written thank you card to me thanking me for the recent purchase. Writing the card probably took the salesperson about two minutes, and the postage cost the company 32 cents. However, this is a very small fee to win over a current customer for a lifetime. The thank-you card helped me have a personal experience with the company. I felt the employees at Ultimate Electronics actually cared I had come into the business. Ultimately, they cared I had helped them stay in business.

APPRECIATION MESSAGES

A note or letter expressing appreciation is always a treat and opportunities for these are almost unlimited. The format is less important than the tone of such a message. In fact, you can often be casual and creative in such messages so long as you project a pleasant tone. Handwritten notes can be as good as formally typed messages. Personal note paper can be used rather than letterhead.

To strengthen a note of appreciation,

1. *Mention or describe the specific actions, attitudes, or characteristics that you appreciate.* Just saying "I appreciate you" is nice. But saying, "I appreciate the way you are open to new ideas" or "I appreciate your help in providing me with . . ." is likely to have more impact.

2. *Use the person's name* in the body of the message. Don't overdo it, though—it may sound patronizing—but do personalize the message. Address the reader as you would when talking to him or her. Use first name, nickname, or more formal address as appropriate. Don't call the reader "Bill" if you would normally call him "Mr. Kosinski."

3. *Do not send mixed strokes.* A goodwill message should be all positive. If you have negative information to convey, save it for a separate message. Do not say, "Tom, you did a really good job on the Wesson negotiations. I'm always proud to have you representing our company. But will you please quit wearing those loud ties? They made your appearance less than businesslike."

> It never hurts to spread a little goodwill. In doing so, be efficient yet personal.

4. *Be conversational.* A goodwill letter should sound the way you would talk. Stuffiness or formality can damage the tone. Contractions (I'm, we'd, etc.) are fine. And even terms that are grammatically "incorrect" can create a pleasant tone ("Way-ta-go!" or "Attaboy!")

The degree of formality you choose will depend on what is comfortable for you. Some people prefer the more formal tone, but many enjoy a more conversational, breezy message.

CONGRATULATIONS OR RECOGNITION MESSAGES

Congratulation messages can follow the same guidelines as appreciation notes, although they may be slightly more formal. Be sure to:

1. *Mention the specific actions you are congratulating* the reader for (graduation from the company's advance training program, promo-

tion to _____, bowling a 300 game, a son's advancement to Eagle Scout, etc.)

2. *Suggest that you understand some of the effort that went into the achievement* ("I know this reflects many hours of hard work," etc.).
3. *Express pride and support as appropriate* ("I'm proud to have worked with you and want you to know you'll have my continued support in your new position").

SYMPATHY OR CONDOLENCES

Sooner or later we all face the experience of sharing grief. We are faced with the need to communicate with those who are dealing with the inevitable process of mourning. It is useful to understand something of the psychology of mourning.

Professor James Calvert Scott explains: "Mourning involves the psychological task of breaking the bonds with that which has been lost and eventually reinvesting that attachment in living people and things. Society's death-related rituals, including the letter of condolence, play a significant role in repairing and restoring the emotional and social damage caused by death."[4]

Well-meaning family and friends often interfere with the grieving process by avoiding mention of the loss at the very time the bereaved need most to confront it. By doing so, they prevent the bereaved from experiencing the reality of death and the full range of emotions that are necessary in order to accomplish a healthy resolution. Working through grief is the process of consciously admitting and accepting the loss intellectually and emotionally. The ultimate goal of grief work is to be able to remember the loss without emotional pain and to direct emotions to the future.[5]

The psychologically sound letter of condolence should help the bereaved to work through their grief. You can accomplish this by following these guidelines:

1. Acknowledge how you learned about and reacted to the death.
2. Avoid euphemisms relating to death and to the deceased person. Refer to him or her by name, not "the dearly departed"; say "died" or "passed away," not "expired."
3. Maintain a sincere, positive tone by focusing on the contributions of the deceased person. Perhaps relate a specific example of how he or she influenced your life.
4. Avoid quoting poetry, rhetorical writing, or scripture unless you are certain that it will bring comfort. Your original thoughts are far more valued.
5. Make a specific offer of assistance, if possible. Offer to help with child care or to house visiting relatives, as appropriate. Anticipate your reader's needs and try to be of service.

GENERAL PATTERN OF GOODWILL MESSAGES

A get-right-to-the-point approach usually works best in goodwill messages. Often the first words will be "congratulations" or "I appreciate" or "I am sorry to hear . . ."

The pattern, format, or even the grammar of a goodwill message is less important than is the fact that it was sent and reflects a sense of caring. Typically a goodwill message will take only a few minutes to produce but will offer a great return in improved relationships.

HOW ORGANIZATIONS CAN CREATE GOODWILL

The "public" form of a goodwill message may take the form of a press release. Here, the intent is to convey good news or to shed light on some positive aspect of an organization via a message broadcast through print or electronic media. Although not personalized, such messages can help create a positive image for the company and attract customers.

GETTING PUBLICITY

A properly produced news release can be the backbone of any publicity campaign or image building effort. While sending out news releases is the most obvious part of getting mentioned in the media, creating real news about your product or service is actually the first step. The next step is identifying and contacting the appropriate media to receive your news release. To get the best results, send your news releases only to those media whose audiences are very likely to be interested in what you have to say.

Follow up any press releases you send to the media.

Follow up often gets overlooked, but it is crucial to any publicity campaign. Make follow-up phone calls to the media contacts to make sure they received your release, but don't try to pressure them into running it. If they run it, be sure to thank them. If they don't run it, don't call and complain.

If you're certain your releases would be of interest to a certain medium's audience, keep sending them new information and following up. The more releases you send, the more likely one of them will eventually be run. Don't get discouraged, just keep trying. If your releases are newsworthy, with enough patience and persistence, you'll get them placed.

THE NEWS RELEASE

The basic tool for generating publicity (i.e., public goodwill) is the news release. With it companies can get free publicity from newspapers, magazines, radio, and television. Most of the news in newspapers and magazines comes from news releases sent out by companies, government agencies, associations, and various individuals and groups.

> News releases provide much of the information found in the media.

Since a properly prepared news release is the cornerstone of any publicity campaign, be sure that you create a good one. While some room for creativity exists, a common, easy-to-follow format is used for most successful news releases. It has several key elements: the originator (you), the release date, the contact, a headline, and the double-spaced copy itself.

If you send out the news release on your company stationery, that will take care of the originator. All you have to do is type NEWS or NEWS RELEASE in capital letters at the top of the letterhead. The release date is the date you want the story released. In many cases, it can say FOR IMMEDIATE RELEASE. This is probably best, unless there is some overriding reason why the story can't be released before a certain date. Also necessary is the name and telephone number of a person to contact for further information.

The headline should appear in capital letters, six spaces below the contact line. It should be as clever and catchy as possible so it captures the attention and arouses the interest of the editor or producer. Newspaper headlines can be used as models of how to write news release headlines. Try for a headline that compels the reader to read the entire release.

Eight spaces below the headline, you should begin the body of the release. It should be double-spaced and written like a newspaper article, with the most important information in the first paragraph, the supporting information next, and the least important information last. A news release can be any length, but a one-page release is probably best. If you do use more than one page, place the word "MORE" at the bottom center of the first page.

You can use news releases to announce the start of your company, new products and services, speaking engagements, and appearances on radio or television shows, or any other event connected with your company that has potential news value.

Whom you address your news releases to is extremely important. Newspapers and magazines have specialized editors, while each radio and television talk show has a specific producer. Your best chance for getting the publicity you desire is by directing your release to the appropriate editor or producer.

Because your release may be reprinted verbatim in some newspapers or organizational newsletters, spend ample time to compose clever, readable releases. In some cases, your release may even be used as the basis for a feature story.

It's a good idea for your news releases to end with a "For more information" paragraph. Give your company's name, address, and phone number and offer a free brochure or some other kind of promotional material. Doing this encourages people to contact your business, giving you new prospects and an opportunity to gauge the relative impact of that particular coverage.

> A press release (or news release) can be a great way to inform customers and potential customers about the goings-on in your company.

A FINAL THOUGHT

Written communication is often overlooked as a customer service tool. Many people are uncomfortable writing, but by applying some simple techniques such as those discussed in this chapter, they can use the power of written messages to build customer relationships. Comedian Woody Allen once said the "80 percent of all success is just showing up." I think that's largely true. And when it comes to using written messages for customer service, 80 percent of your success will be in simply doing it! Don't be overly worried about the "correctness" of your writing; just write the way you'd talk and let the customer know that you care enough to send a written message.

-------------------- *Summary of Key Ideas* --------------------

▶ Written messages are an often-overlooked tool for creating customer satisfaction and loyalty.

▶ Goodwill notes are those you send even though you don't have to. Their power arises from customers' surprise at receiving them.

▶ Originality helps boost the power of goodwill messages. Almost everybody sends Christmas cards; be more creative and you'll get greater impact.

▶ Be direct and straightforward in routine messages. Get right to the point.

▶ Create goodwill via news releases about the organization.

Application Activity

Prepare a Generic Customer Thank You Note

Using the guidelines in this chapter, draft a thank you note that could be used for immediate follow-up with your customers. (Use an imaginary business if you are not currently employed.) Leave blank spaces where others in your organization could fill in details as they use the same format for thank you notes.

Application Activity

Prepare a Practice News Release

Using the guidelines in this section, write a brief news release from "You, Inc." Announce a significant achievement or bit of information about you. (Don't worry too much about news worthiness at this point. Our purpose is to practice the news release format.)

NOTES

[1] Some of the material in this chapter is adopted from P. R. Timm and J. A. Stead, *Communication Skills for Business and Professions* (Upper Saddle River, NJ: Prentice Hall, 1996), especially Chapter 10.

[2] Ibid., p. 259.

[3] Transmitted via America Online, November 4, 1992.

[4] Calvert, J. S., "Teaching Business Students to Write the Psychologically Sound Letter of Condolence," an unpublished paper written at Utah State University. 1984.

[5] Ibid.

The One-to-One Customer Future[1]

Changing conventions in customer service

Your entire future lies ahead of you.

—basketball coach Jim Valvano

THE WAY IT IS . . . BACK FROM THE FUTURE[2]

In late 1991 the telegraph industry's life was taken, suddenly and brutally, by the facsimile machine. For more than 150 years, the telegram stood for immediacy and importance. It was an icon for urgency. But now, Western Union has closed down its telegraph service around the world. The fax was a new technology the telegram could not survive.

The shift from teletype and telegram to facsimile transmission represents one aspect of what some business consultants term a "paradigm shift"—a discontinuity in the otherwise steady march of business progress.

The automobile was another discontinuity, one that radically transformed both the economy and society. When the automobile first appeared, it seemed to be merely a horseless version of the well-known carriage. Predicting the consequences of the automobile's introduction would have been nearly impossible. Who would have imagined that a noisy, smelly, unreliable machine would eventually be responsible for the creation of suburbs; the fractionalization of families; and the growth of supermarkets, malls, and the interstate highway system?

Today we are passing through a technological discontinuity of epic proportions, and most of us are not even remotely prepared. The old paradigm, a system of mass production, mass media, and mass marketing, is being replaced by a totally new paradigm, a one-to-one economic system.

The one-to-one future will be characterized by customized production, individually addressable media, and one-to-one marketing, totally changing the rules of business competition and growth. Instead of market share, the goal of most business competition will be share of the customer—one customer at a time.

> Successful businesses of the future will focus not on market share as much as share of the customer.

Having the size necessary to produce, advertise, and distribute vast quantities of standardized products won't be a precondition for success. Instead, products will be increasingly tailored to individual tastes, electronic media will be inexpensively addressed to individual consumers, and many products ordered over the phone will be delivered to the home in eight hours or less.

In the one-to-one future, businesses will focus on the kinds of profits that can be realized from long-term customer retention and lifetime values.

The discontinuity we are now living through will be every bit as disruptive to our lives, and as beneficial, as the Industrial Revolution was to the lives of our great-grandparents. The way we compete will change dramatically enough over just the next few years to alter the very structure of our society, empowering some and disenfranchising others.

The one-to-one future holds immense implications for individual privacy, social cohesiveness, and the alienation and fractionalization that could come from the breakdown of mass media. It will change forever how we seek our information, education, and entertainment, and how we pursue our happiness. In addition to the "haves" and "have nots," new class distinctions will be created between the "theres" and "there nots." Some people will have jobs that require them to *be there*—somewhere—while others will be able to work mostly from their homes, without having to be anywhere.

It would be difficult to underestimate the cataclysmic changes that will jolt society as a result of this paradigm shift. It will disrupt everything, but ultimately one-to-one technology will create an entrepreneurial froth of opportunities. When the dust has settled, new businesses—millions of them—most not even conceived today, will have sprung up across the economic landscape as naturally and randomly as wild flowers after a severe winter.

In a world in which communication and information are practically free, the economic system will be driven more than ever before by genuine innovation and human creativity. In such a world, ideas will be the medium of exchange.[3]

-------------------- *Learning Objectives* --------------------

After you have studied this chapter you should be able to

1. Describe the major changes occurring in today's business world that result in significantly increased individual attention to customers.

2. Apply the one-to-one marketing principle to the process of building customer satisfaction and loyalty.

3. Recognize the impact of technological, social, and economic changes and adapt your career to meet these changes.

4. Understand how communication media and increased interactivity will have a dramatic impact on customers.

5. Apply principles of relationship marketing and contact management systems to customer service.

6. Recognize that ultimately, career success arises from fulfilling a stewardship for giving great service and building customer loyalty.

TECHNOLOGY SHIFTS FOR THE NEW FUTURE

The demise of the telegraph industry is, of course, only one of countless examples of so called paradigm shifts—new ways of thinking about and doing business. The list of obsolete products and services replaced by new, previously unimagined ones is long. And the pace of these changes seems ever-increasing. Even the youngest reader of this book can likely recall 1980. Yet many of us forget today's commonplace devices that were not yet used then. For example, there were no automatic teller machines, laser printers, or cellular phones. But even more incredible, "the number of televisions with remote control

> Technology has changed our lives dramatically in the past few decades.

devices was statistically insignificant. There were no compact disks, almost no videocassette recorders, and no video rental stores. Only restaurants had microwave ovens. Facsimile machines cost several thousand dollars each, took five minutes or more to transmit a single page, and were found only in very large companies. No one had a personal computer."[4]

It's easy to find examples of technology that seem to reflect huge changes in our way of life. But, perhaps just as significant have been the social, economic, and political shifts that impact business, the professions, and customer satisfaction.

SOCIAL AND ECONOMIC SHIFTS
FOR THE NEW FUTURE

Aside from technology, other noteworthy changes affect business and and customer relationships today. On the social and economic scene we see substantial demographic shifts. Work forces are increasingly diverse—made up of people from a wide range of economic circumstances, cultures, religions, and both genders. Working couples have come to value shopping efficiency and convenience. Ethnically diverse neighborhoods have caused restaurants serving many kinds of foods to flourish. Fast food and take-home cuisine have become the mainstay of some busy families. Today's work force consists of more two-income families and single parents with the associated family responsibilities this poses. We have an increasingly educated work force and its people are less tolerant of mindless, repetitive work. People today expect to be more involved in organizational decisions, to have their input considered.

All these people are, of course, customers. Their shifting social conditions have stimulated demand for new and different products and services.

Politically, organizations face increasing government regulations, most of which reflect political mandates not previously considered in the business world. Equal employment opportunities for people of all backgrounds, persons with disabilities, and gender equity are among the more notable changes of recent years. Likewise concern for the environment, employee health and safety, and even emotional well being have become hallmarks of today's successful businesses. Caring companies attract and keep better employees (internal customers) and ultimately succeed in the marketplace. Most companies are aware of "green" issues: recycling and ecologically friendly packaging. In short, customers have come to expect different kinds of satisfaction.

NEW MEDIA FOR A ONE-TO-ONE FUTURE

The ways we communicate, especially the media we can use, have made big differences in the ways organizations interact among their own members and with the world outside. In addition to the obvious speed and efficiency advantages of today's media, there are other considerations that have an impact on customer relationships. One of the most significant trends is in the increasing ability to efficiently generate personalized, one-to-one messages tailored to the needs and wants of individuals, especially customers, co-workers, and associates.

> One-to-one, individually tailored messages can now be sent to huge audiences.

Communication experts have long recognized that the more we know about our message receiver, and the more we personalize a message to the receiver's wants and interests, the more effective we will be in communicating and building relationships.

Customized messages aimed at individual readers are a powerful tool in business as well as personal communication. In an organization's marketing function, for example, we are seeing a shift from mass marketing—sending the same messages to a massive number of people in hopes that some of them will respond favorably—to individualized marketing where we send a unique individualized message to each person. This personalization began with word processing which gave us the ability to merge letters that include personalized sections interspersed with the generic message.

Today, mass mailers routinely take advantage of this ability to personalize sales letters, sweepstakes entry forms, and even the envelopes they are sent in. But today's media let us go far beyond what has been done in the past. Now we can include past buying information and personal preferences and convey a sense that we know and understand our reader.

> Today's media go beyond the simple merging of names and addresses.

With the help of technology, we are progressively moving toward what Don Pepper and Martha Rogers, the authors of our opening segment, call one-to-one marketing. The intent of one-to-one marketing is to create long term *relationships* with customers and to provide for a wide range of their needs. With mass marketing and it's communication media such as mass media ads or junk mail, the goal has been to gain a larger *share of the market*. If, for example, your store accounts for 10 percent of all the men's wear sold in your town, mass marketing will try to get that up to 12 or 15 percent. The assumption is, of course, that a larger share of market means more profits. Unfortunately, this is becoming less of a sure thing. Advertising costs have increased and results have dropped. It costs more and more money to get a new customer into your business using traditional approaches.

The one-to-one marketing instead focuses on establishing an ongoing relationship with existing customers. You do this by gathering as much information about them as possible and responding to their needs. A men's wear store today may do very little mass advertising and still be very profitable by keeping close to its customers and meeting all their clothing needs. A bank or credit union may expand its services to eventually handle all its customers' financial needs. This is called

> One-to-one marketing builds relationships that allow businesses to earn a larger share of the customer's business.

getting a larger *share of the customer* and has been found to be very profitable.

Interactivity Options Now Available

Today's technology makes the one-to-one process possible. In the past, keeping track of customer names and addresses, sales data, and personal preferences was a complex and time-consuming process. Many people have kept such customer data on 3 x 5 cards in a file box. As the number of customers grew, the task became impractical. Today's computers and point-of-sale electronic data gathering devices, however, make it easy. We can now track individual preferences, poll customers about their needs, and customize services and products to meet those needs. Many stores are now offering discount coupons to the customer at the checkout counter. If the customer buys a six-pack of Pepsi, the scanner generates a coupon for 50-cents off on Frito-Lay potato chips. (Frito-Lay is a division of PepsiCo.)

Interactivity between a business and its customers will now let consumers instantly respond to advertisements through their TV sets and computers. This technology has advertisers scurrying around looking for opportunities to experiment, according to marketing executives. There is a huge future in interactive advertising, only no one knows when the future starts, says Irving A. Miller of Toyota Motor Sales USA.[5] I'll talk more about cyberspace and interactive buying later in this chapter.

The one-to-one principle holds for internal customer relationships too. Managers who keep closely attuned to their employees' preferences, talents, and wants build long-term relationships that can be mutually beneficial to the company. A fully utilized employee is the counterpart to the fully served customer.

On the social, friendship level, knowing about and addressing the interests, needs, and wants of friends have always been major factors in building rapport and life-long relationships. Interactivity—the two way flow of information—is the key.

Many effective networkers keep reminder data on friends and acquaintances. We know a highly successful business entrepreneur who, from the earliest days of his career, kept an index card on each person he met. On the card he would jot notes about the person's family, interests, pets, birth dates and anniversaries, accomplishments—even favorite jokes. Then, each time he spoke on the phone, he'd pull out the person's card

> One-to-one interactivity applies equally well to internal customers and even personal friendships.

and use ideas from it in the conversation. That's one-to-one communication. And today's media magnify this ability.

MEDIA BREAKTHROUGHS ALLOW MORE ONE-TO-ONE COMMUNICATION

Today's communication media typically combine the power of computers to allow such one-to-one relationship building on a larger scale. These media have the following characteristics:

1. They are *individually addressable and highly adaptive* to unique needs. They permit messages to be fully tailored to each customer, not just superficially modified versions of a form letter.
2. They are *interactive*, creating two-way, not one-way communication. They make it easy for customers to give their feedback and reactions to messages.
3. They are *affordable and powerful.*

   Are such media available to the typical business person or professional? More than any time in history, the answer is an unqualified yes. Even the smallest business or individual proprietorship can afford much of today's technology. We are steadily moving toward more effective one-to-one service in business and the professions, supported by electronic media that can individualize messages.

CHANGING THE OLD CONVENTIONS

You probably have heard someone describe a super salesperson as one who can sell anything to anyone—even ice cubes to an igloo inhabitant in Alaska. The old convention taught that dynamic sales skills are the ticket to success. If the salesperson could give a decent presentation of the product and slam the consumer with an amazing close, then the consumer would buy. That was it. Transaction complete.

   In our day, a new convention is on the rise. Although presentation and closing are still important to the sales process, an even more vital element supersedes both of these—the customer's satisfaction. Today's consumers face an unprecedented number of choices. Because of our free enterprise system, consumers have hundreds of places to go to buy the very same product. What makes the customer choose which place of business to buy from? Are choices based on quality, price, convenience, or on customer service? How do you decide where to buy clothes, groceries, automobiles, electronics, and other consumer goods? What is most important to you as a consumer? There is no mystery in the answers to these questions. A consumer will go where the most is offered—the most value, most efficient systems, and most pleasant and personable transactions. It is that simple.

RELATIONSHIP MARKETING: THE ONLY WAY TO SURVIVE IN THE FUTURE

Companies may argue they have the best quality product around at great prices. The fact is, customers have gotten used to having quality products at good prices. These things are givens. They alone cannot readily distinguish one business from the competition.

> Customers in a free-market economy expect good products at reasonable cost. This is a given. What they don't always expect is great service.

But customers have learned by experience to expect less than excellent service. Why? Because that is what they've been getting in the past. Can you see the great opportunity that exists for a strong competitive advantage?

Think back to when you were a child. Do you remember a corner grocer, or a candy store manager? Did he know who you were or who your parents were? A typical comment from the grocer might have been, "Hi Billy, it's good to see you. Did you have a good trip to the Grand Canyon?" Or from the candy store manager, "Hello Susie, last time you were here you bought those chewy licorice drops. Can I get you the same thing, or would you like to try something different?" This is relationship marketing—having a one-to-one relationship with your customers. Every company—from a *Fortune 500* to a local baby-sitter—can utilize relationship marketing with just a bit of training. In fact, relationship marketing is only limited by the creativity of the people in the company.

> Relationship marketing opportunities are limited only by one's imagination.

With the use of creativity, the opportunity to exceed customers' expectations extends well beyond just calling someone by name. That is a great start, but consider the following example given by Michael Gerber in his book, *The E Myth Revisited* to see how far superior service can be taken:

On his way back to his home in San Francisco from a business trip, Michael decided to stop for the night in a little hotel overlooking the Pacific. When he arrived at the reception desk, quickly a well-dressed woman appeared and welcomed him to the hotel. Within three minutes from the greeting, he was ushered into his room by the bell boy. The room was decorated with plush carpeting, white-on-white bedding, natural cedar walls, and a stone fireplace.

The fireplace grate had oak logs, rolled paper, and matches waiting to be used.

After changing in his room, Michael walked to the restaurant. The hotel receptionist had made him reservations for the restaurant at the time of his check-in. Michael was immediately shown to his table upon arrival—even though others without reservations were waiting. When he got back to his room that night, the pillows were plumped up, the bed was turned down and there was a fire blazing in the fireplace. On the night stand was a glass of brandy and a card that read, "Welcome to your first stay at Venetia. I hope it has been enjoyable. If there is anything I can do for you, day or night, please don't hesitate to call. Kathi."

In the morning Michael woke up to the smell of coffee. When he went into the bathroom he found a perking coffee pot. A card by the pot read, "Your brand of coffee. Enjoy! K." Michael had been asked the night before at the restaurant which brand of coffee he preferred. Now it was bubbling in his room. Michael heard a polite knock on the door. When he opened the door, he saw the *New York Times* laying on the mat. When Michael had checked in, the reservationist had asked him what paper he preferred. Now his preferred paper was at his room for him to read.

Michael explains the service at the hotel has been exactly the same every time he has gone back. But after the first visit, he was never asked his preferences again.[6]

This is a great example of relationship marketing and of customer service. By "learning" his preferences, the hotel management was able to manipulate a common experience into one that was very personal for Michael—exceeding any expectations he might have had. To be successful relationship marketers, you must become personal with your customers. After having a personalized experience with a business, a customer becomes very loyal. Think about it—would you patronize another hotel in the area after having a similar experience? Why would anyone want to take the chance of getting the "expected" service of any other hotel? You can begin to see why relationship marketing is so powerful and so correlated with customer service.

GAINING CUSTOMER SHARE; NOT MARKET SHARE

Let's talk once again about the important concept of *customer share*. Progressive companies are coming to see the wisdom of focusing on share of customers rather than share of market.[7] Consider the following two competing flower businesses:

- The owners of flower Company A have worked very hard, with a mass-marketing focus, in order to get a good piece of the market.

They calculated that Company A has about 20 percent market share. In other words, for every dollar spent on flowers in the market, Company A gets 20 cents.

- The owners of flower Company B, on the other hand, have worked very hard to gain a relationship with every one of the top purchasers of flowers (those who buy flowers on the most consistent basis). They estimate that they have a 20 percent customer share. That is, for every 10 customers who buy flowers, 2 of them buy flowers from Company B 100 percent of the time.

Which company is better off in the long run? Remember who Company B focused on—the customers who are frequent buyers—the top customers of the industry. Therefore, Company B enjoys much greater efficiency in their marketing—its customers are the best customers to have. They know them and they have massaged their relationship to gain even more of their flower business. They win.

> Companies that win the loyalty of their top customers will be more efficient and profitable than those who chase a continuing flow of new customers.

If a company can win over the top customers, then its chance of survival is much better than just having a percentage of the market. Managers need to think of the present value of a customer's future business. An example illustrates what I mean: In the book, *Customers for Life*, by Carl Sewell and Paul B. Brown, Carl explains the importance of thinking about the present value of future business.[8] Carl owns one of the largest luxury car dealerships in the country. He has calculated that every customer has the potential of bringing his dealership $332,000 in sales. If an average luxury car costs about $25,000, and if people buy on average 12 cars, then the total sale is $300,000. Add service and parts and each customer of Carl's dealership is worth about $332,000 in sales.

Mark Grainer, chairman of the Technical Assistance Research Programs Institute (TARP), similarly estimates that a loyal supermarket customer is worth $3,800 annually.[9] Over the course of a lifetime, this could easily add up to more than $150,000 in sales. Furthermore, a businessperson who flies frequently to different parts of the world could easily spend over $50,000 annually on air travel. This customer could be worth over one million dollars in revenue for an airline! This is what we mean by present value of future business.

> Present value of future business is an estimate of the total a customer would potentially spend with you over a lifetime.

With this kind of long-range dollar thinking, who wouldn't give priority to customer share rather than a market share? The customer you already have is infinitely more likely to buy from you again, while ever scrambling for new customers drains your marketing budget and energy. Remember, though, the only way to increase customer share is to build a relationship with your customer and to enhance your customer's satisfaction and loyalty.

DATABASE MARKETING: AN INTEGRAL PART OF FUTURE CUSTOMER SERVICE

Every day thousands of inventions are registered. Occasionally, one of these inventions changes the way businesses do things forever. Just 15 years ago, most businesses were without personal computers. In our day, however, computers have become a common "must have" for every type of business.

Because of computers, we are able to store great amounts of detailed information and retrieve any of this information in just seconds. The computer has greatly enhanced the possibilities for any company to begin relationship marketing and increase customer service. When managers collect information, they put the information into a database. This database can be accessed in the future to retrieve any of this information.

Databases of customer information are invaluable in building business relationships.

Successful business people have always used databases—the ones in their heads. Remember the corner grocer and the candy store manager? They knew most of their customers' names, and they probably even knew what each customer purchased the last time he or she was in the store. They stored this kind of information in their mind—their most important database. When businesses began to get larger, managers started writing pertinent information down. This information would be filed away and located at a later time. Today, most companies input this information into computer databases. The database saves space, time, and over the long run, money. That is what computers do best: remember things.

USING DATABASE IN A BUSINESS

An excellent use of a computer database can be seen at some electronic super stores. These leading edge retailers use technology to find and store information about each customer. When you first walk into the door of such a store, an employee at a desk will ask if you have become a member. If you have not, then you give the employee some basic information such as name, address, and telephone number. In return the employee gives you a plastic card to carry in your wallet. You have now become a "member" of the retailer's "family." This painless registration process starts giving the store *incredible* amounts of information. Every time you now go into the store, an employee scans your membership card with a barcode scanner. Don't worry if you have forgotten your card. The employee at the desk can easily look up your number. When a customer purchases something the membership card is again scanned.

With the use of this database, the managers know exactly when and how many times you went to their store. They know what you bought on each visit and the items you are most interested in. This information is extremely valuable and can be used for different reasons. For example, when you go to the checkout stand, the employee can immediately get your information, call you by name, and ask, "has the CD player you bought two weeks ago been working well for you?"

With the database of information, the managers at such a store can also market directly to those who would benefit most from the marketing. For instance, suppose the managers have received word from Hewlett Packard that a ten-dollar customer rebate will be given for each Hewlett Packard ink cartridge sold. The store can then send a mailing to anyone who has bought a Hewlett Packard printer or Hewlett Packard printer supplies within the last five years. With this information, the store can market to individuals or, in other words, utilize relationship marketing. The customers see this as great customer service—they only get the coupons and ads they are personally interested in.

Service Snapshot

The Reminder

Thanks to computer databases, Fischer Florist in Atlantic City, New Jersey, is able to collect information and use it for retention of customers.[10] Every day the managers at Fischer Florist send out reminder cards to certain customers. A reminder card may read as follows:

> Dear Mr. Jones: On March 29, last year, you remembered Jenny's birthday by sending her one dozen roses. Enclosed is a catalog of other beautiful flowers we offer. Please call our toll-free telephone number to place an order. We will make sure Jenny has your choice of flowers on that special day. Thank you for your business. We look forward to hearing from you.

When Mr. Jones calls, he must only tell the flower shop what flowers to send. Jenny's address, telephone number, and available times for delivery are already in the computer database. Likewise, Mr. Jones' credit card number is on file and can easily be confirmed and used.

Think how you could E-Plus even these techniques. Why not do as one gift catalog company has done in using its database. The company implemented a new program that offers the following services:[11] They will

1. Send any number of gifts to your friends and relatives when you order them from the catalog up to 15 months in advance.
2. Deliver the gift on the day specified on the order form. The customer will never again miss any important date.
3. Bill the customer's credit card only when the gifts are sent. Send an invoice to the customer for each gift charged to the account within 5 working days.
4. Send a reminder postcard to the customer before the gift is sent out explaining who the gift is going to and what the gift is.
5. Send all customers an updated catalog periodically. This new catalog will have all of the previous years names preprinted on the order sheet, and the customer can add any new names on the bottom.
6. Provide a 24-hour toll-free telephone number for any changes or updates the customer may have.

With the use of a database, the information needed to do all this is stored easily; and the catalog store employees most likely have less work than they did before the service was implemented. Best of all, the managers can see almost exactly what their sales revenue will be in the near future, thus helping financial planning for the company.

To add an interactive dimension to this service, the company includes two short questions on the customer order form. They ask the customers what they would like to see our catalog service include in the future? And what are some additional products you would like us to have in our gift catalog? Bingo! Customer preferences and expectations are revealed and E-Plus opportunities become clear.

USING CONTACT MANAGEMENT SYSTEMS

Contact management is the process of managing, tracking, and organizing contacts with your customers and potential customers. This has been standard procedure for physicians who have always been expected to record information about any patient visit. Many doctors dictate the information on a tape recorder and then have a secretary type the record later. This is a form of contact management. But it's not just for physicians any more. Imagine the following scenario:

You walk into work one morning. Your secretary tells you one of your customers named John is on the phone. John wants to know if the delivery time of two weeks is still possible. John also forgot the prices and quantities you had quoted him and would like to get them now before he goes into his meeting in five minutes. "Wow," you think to yourself, "which customer is John anyway?" Finally, you find the two different files John's information is in and you pick up the phone to call him back. Just then a customer walks into your office and says to you, "Where were you? You were supposed to come to my office and present your product to the Board of Trustees this morning. I'm sorry but I don't think you will be good enough to get the contract."

With better contact management the unfortunate scenario can be resolved. The idea of contact management is to record every important detail of any communication with the customer. This information may include price quotes, dates of last contacts, dates of future meetings, promises made, reminders of any special information, letters or advertisements sent, and so on. This information must be organized and filed in some way such that it is readily available. Today, companies are using computerized contact-management software to do this.

The software allows you to file away great amounts of information that can be brought up in seconds. For example, if the phone rings and John is on the phone, you can open any file with the name "John" and see exactly who he is, what you have promised him, when you are supposed to contact him next, and what you should be talking to him about. Most software programs allow you to search all customers for general information as well. For example, if you like to be proactive and contact your customers on a regular basis, contact management software, can search for those customers that have not been called for at least two weeks.

> Contact-management software can be of tremendous value to virtually any business.

Because you can readily access information about your customer, you can build a stronger relationship. For instance, if a customer mentions that she is going out to dinner (say, at Chuckie-Cheeze Pizza House!) for her daughter's birthday, you can add a note in your contact management software. The next time you talk with this customer you can ask, "How was your daughter's birthday dinner?" Questions like this will get a customer thinking about you as a concerned friend, not just another person trying to sell her something.

Although large companies may use highly specialized, custom contact-management software, most of us can use software that is sold at any local software store. There is no reason for a small company to spend thousands of dollars having contact manager software or database software custom made. Action Plus, Sales Ally, Bizbase Gold, Maximizer, and ACT 2.0 are all good contact managers that suit the needs of most businesses and only cost between $70 and $500.

Service Snapshot

Special Service for Best Customers

Hertz Car Rental knew they had problems when people were getting upset about having to wait in long lines to get their rental cars. Many businesspeople travel on very tight schedules and need to have a car quickly. Hertz knew that unless some action was taken quickly, they would lose many of their most valuable and frequent renters. Hertz launched a special service, the #1 Gold Club, for those who needed their rental cars quickly. The #1 Gold Club members can call ahead of time to reserve a car. When the member gets off the plane, a shuttle is waiting for the customer at the curb to take him or her to the car. The shuttle driver can welcome him or her by name and explain that the shuttle trip is just 2 minutes. The shuttle drops the customer off at the reserved car. The engine is running, the trunk lid is open, and today's issue of the *Wall Street Journal* is on the front seat. The member gets in the car, drives to the gate, shows his or her driver's license and #1 Gold Card. No lines. No hassle.

THE ELECTRONIC FUTURE

Predicting the future in an ever-changing world is, of course, impossible. However, we can be sure to expect some application of new technologies like these:

Internet Shopping. Companies of all sizes and shapes are scrambling to get a "home page." A user of the Internet from anywhere in the world can dial up this home page and receive product information, prices, instructions, and even coupons. Right now the Internet is still a novelty—and a test market—for most companies. In the future we can count on every business marketing on the Internet. In fact, one day Internet access will be as common as the telephone.

Virtual Reality Shopping. Another use of technology may be a few years behind today's 'net shopping. Imagine yourself at your home and the weekly chore of grocery shopping has come again. You walk over to your computer and put on a pair of virtual reality (VR) glasses. You dial up the local grocery store and start perusing the aisles—just as if you were there. In your VR glasses you see the grocery aisles and can maneuver your "virtual" self down the aisles. No traffic. No carts to bump into. Just you with free run of the grocery store. With your VR joystick you reach out and put the groceries you would like into your virtual basket. When you are done with your shopping, you reach out with your virtual arm and touch the sign that says done. Within an hour the groceries are delivered to your home.

Can you imagine the customer-service opportunities companies will have with this technology? With just the use of computer programs, stores could individualize every aspect according to the customer's preferences. Let's take the above example a bit further.

While you are shopping in the VR store you decide you would like to buy that six-pack of Pepsi I talked about earlier. This time, instead of getting a Frito-Lay coupon, you see Greg, the "Virtual" Coca-Cola stocker. He hands you a 50-cents-off coupon for a six-pack of *Coca- Cola*. All you need to do if you would like to automatically switch brands and save 50 cents is reach out and take the VR coupon. That'll tick off the Pepsi people, but it's an example of the increasing competitiveness in our VR world.

Imagine one more use of VR. You are interested in moving to California. You sit down at your computer and do a search for companies who build houses in California. You find a company and E-mail them some things you're looking for in a home. Within hours you go back to their "site" on the Internet, put on your VR glasses and take a "virtual" walk through the exact home you ordered. If you don't like it, you make some changes. When your house is exactly the way you like it, you start taking virtual tours of locations for your home. Finally, you order your custom-designed house that you have seen—even though it does not exist yet!

Interactive TV. Another important technological change will be the change in television. Right now a consumer is forced to watch what they want to watch at certain times. Soon we can expect interactive television. If you want to watch an episode of *60 Minutes*, you will be able to order it and watch it at your convenience. You will have the option to watch shows free of charge with commercials, or watch shows for a very small fee without commercials. Since advertisements on television shows today generate about 25 cents in revenue per watcher per show, some experts predict the cost of watching a show would be just 25 cents or so.

Interactive television offers much more than convenience in watching television shows. Everyone with a video camera will ultimately have the opportunity to get into viewers' homes. Just as anyone now can have a home page on the Internet, anyone in the future will be able to have a television show or television commercial. As consumers, we will dial up these commercials when we need a specific product or service. For example, if you're looking for a new car, you would just have to search the database for video information on vehicles. You will be able to watch information from BMW, GM, Ford, Acura, and from all other automobile companies. You will also be able to get video information about your neighbor down the street who is selling her 1996 red BMW 325i convertible.

With interactive television, the consumers will be in control of the information they receive. The broadcaster will just make the information available. Similarly, there will be no more junk mail, no more unwanted advertisements coming into the consumer's home. The consumer will select only the companies which he or she wants to get information from. Thus ultimately the consumer will decide which company to start a relationship with.

These are just a few of the examples of what the future holds. Few people doubt that the future will dramatically change the way we do business forever.

TECHNOLOGY IS GREAT, BUT ULTIMATELY WE FACE THE QUESTION OF STEWARDSHIP

This chapter focused on some future tactics, many of which center around technology. In closing this book, however, I'd like to stress another point. Ultimately your career success and success in applying the process of customer service will depend upon your attitudes toward *stewardship*. Stewardship means to hold in trust the well-being of some larger entity—our organization, our community, the earth itself. Peter Block, author of a book entitled *Stewardship,* reminds us that we will always face a tug-of-war between service and self-interest. Below is a brief essay developed from Block's ideas. Please read it carefully and think about how you can apply its ideas to the process of customer service.[12]

Another Look
Choosing Service over Self-Interest

A Model of Stewardship

The idea of service through stewardship has been with us forever. Corporate stewardship has come to mean financial responsibility for both the institution and the community. Stewardship, though, goes beyond financial accountability and beyond being accountable for our talents. Stewardship is also concerned with the use of power. One intent of stewardship is to replace self-interest with service as the basis for holding and using power.

It is not surprising we should look to religious models for ways of thinking about the right use of power. Our best religious leaders have flourished through the ages in part because they have understood how to exercise accountability and activism in service to their followers. Mahatma Gandhi is one of the best examples of integrating the religious and the political so well. Gandhi identified three elements making up his brand of service-based power, which he called trusteeship. Granted, Gandhi sets a rather high standard, but his principles expand our understanding of stewardship's political meaning.

• *Power is granted from those below.* The community creates the chance for a person to be in a position of power. Power is bestowed upon us by those we "lead." We do not claim power; it is not passed on to us by others in power; we have no inherent right to power, whether by birthright, talent, or even achievement. If we serve those who put us in our position, then the recipients of our service and trusteeship are the core workers, the community, and the ones we become accountable to. We may be appointed by a board, or an executive, but they are given their authority as much by the people doing the work as by any other set of owners.

• *Our contribution is our humanity.* The obligation of accepting a position of power is to be, above all else, a good human being. Not to be a good leader, not so much to maintain order and fight back chaos, not to know what is best for others—these are the qualities of being a good parent. If you are a boss, the people working for you definitely have expectations of you to be their good parent, but this is not stewardship.

Stewardship is the willingness to work on ourselves first, to stay in intimate contact with those around us, to own our doubts and limitations, and make them part of our dialogue with others. Our humanness is defined more by our vulnerability than our strengths. This is different from leading from the heart, walking our talk, or articulating a vision.

• *What is true is known to each of us.* Trust comes out of pursuing what is true. What is true lies within each of us. Stewardship is founded on the belief that others have the knowledge and the answers within themselves. We do not have to teach other adults how to behave.

Our survival depends on our taking the idea of service to constituents and making it concrete in our governance systems. The quality and customer service movement has the right idea but is implementing it through patriarchal governance strategies. Service-based governance strategies mean the redistribution of power, privilege, purpose, and wealth. All the team building, improvement teams, and skills training in the world will not create service if the institutional questions of choice and equity never change. Organizations have a hard time taking advantage of their own successful experiments. It would force them to redistribute power and ultimately privilege.

Teaching Revolution to the Ruling Class

We serve when we build capability in others by supporting ownership and choice at every level. We cannot continue to govern through patriarchy and say we just want to be of service. When we act to create compliance in others, we are choosing self-interest over service, no matter what words we use to describe our actions. Service-givers who maintain dominance, aren't. Stewardship at the organizational level has to directly address the redistribution of power, and the redesign of fundamental management practices. Not for their own sake, but in service of the redistribution of felt ownership and felt responsibility.

We are, in fact, talking about a revolution. Revolution means a turn-ing, changing direction, revolving. It means the change required is significant, obvious to the casual observer, even to customers. Evolu-tionary change is more comfortable. Evolutionary change means every-thing is planned, under control, and reasonably predictable. The problem with evolutionary change is that it is virtually unnoticeable to the participants. You have to look back over generations to see any dif-ference. If you want to make changes that go unrecognized, pick an evolutionary path. Patriarchy's attempts to change itself have been traditionally evolutionary, the choice of self-interest.

The revolution is for organizations to become the place where our personal values and economics intersect, reforming our organizations so that our spirit is answered, and our ability to serve customers in the broadest sense is guaranteed. Stewardship is the strategy that embodies this goal. Stewardship enables the use of power with grace.

What is unique about this revolution—and gives us hope—is that it is being initiated by the ruling class, the managerial class. Stewardship is a revolution initiated and designed by those in power.

A FINAL THOUGHT

The future looks exciting for businesses, but most companies will need to make some major changes to be competitive—or they may decide to keep doing things the old fashioned, down-home way they do now. That's an alternative strategy that may appeal to people who don't much care for all this "new-fangled" stuff.

Whatever strategy is chosen, one-to-one customer service and rela-tionship building must stand as its cornerstone. Your willingness to accept the stewardship for producing service excellence will have a direct bearing upon your career success. Apply the ideas in this book and you will succeed.

Another Look

Advanced Technologies Change Perceptions about One-Size-Fits-All Products and Services[13]

It used to be enough to provide a product or service that met a variety of needs for a majority of customers at a rate that kept pace with demand: mass production. Customers realized a degree of compromise was to be expected, that a product designed to satisfy their neighbors *and* themselves would leave both wanting in some way, large or small. The rapid influx of technology—information and manufacturing—has changed all that. One size no longer fits all. People are more aware than ever of their options, and of suppliers' increasing ability to meet them. Exit, mass production; enter, mass customization.

Personal Papers

One industry moving quickly to adapt to consumers' demands for customization is the newspaper business. Major dailies, in particular, are creating new ways to meet readers' specific needs through nontraditional printing methods.

The St. Paul Pioneer Press, St. Paul, MN, launched a service called The Line in early April, says Lem Lloyd, new media director. The Line provides access to numerous kinds of information not available in the paper—or in many cases, Lloyd says, anywhere else.

"Our objective was to recycle the vast amount of information we get every day—some of which we use in the newspaper, some of which we don't—into different forms, and make that available for people in the Twin Cities," Lloyd says.

Each day the paper lists a menu of information available through The Line. Readers call a main number and enter four-digit codes from the menu to access sports scores, stock quotes, nature sounds, entertainment reviews, and other materials of specialized interest but, as such, not worthy of coverage in traditional mass media. Some offerings are merely recordings that are up-dated periodically, such as the North Country Almanac, an educational program featuring documentary-style information about various creatures and their habits, along with sound bites of the animals themselves. Others are updated constantly. The stock and mutual fund report, for example, runs only about 15 minutes behind the action on the trading floor.

When news of special consequence occurs, features in the paper on the subject may include The Line's distinctive logo, accompanied by information about a code to dial for more on the subject. The paper's special D-Day retrospective was supported by a collection of 15 recordings pertinent to the battle. Callers could relive FDR's famous address to the nation: "My fellow Americans, last night when I spoke with you about the fall of Rome, I knew at that moment the troops of the United States and our allies were crossing the channel. . ." Also featured: live recordings from various locations such as the deck of a destroyer in the heat of battle, and speeches from political and military figures of the day.

"We listed these throughout the newspaper in different articles on D-Day," Lloyd says, "and then we listed the entire menu in our special Sunday section."

The response is nothing short of phenomenal, Lloyd says, proof of the vacuum the customized service is filling: A recent feature of frog sounds drew 4,000 calls in a single day.

Filling Niches

The Pioneer Press doesn't limit its product and service customization to The Line, however, it also offers readers written transcripts (for a $3 fee; the audio services are free) of items too lengthy for newspaper coverage. Recent examples include the Nixon funeral eulogies, Jackie Onassis' funeral messages and eulogies with a photo, and Nelson Mandela's inaugural speech. Hundreds of readers ordered each, Lloyd says.

"The price just covers it for us," he says, but the effort is not merely one of community service; it's a matter of positioning for future competitiveness. *"It's a way for people to start looking at us as an information store. We're trying to let people have choices about the news they get from us, rather than just offering them one product and saying, 'Here it is, take it or leave it.'* It's a way to be more responsible to our customers, and to let people interact with the newspaper more."

The interaction isn't one-way at the Pioneer Press, Lloyd says. A line is often designated for callers who want direct input on a current issue and may actually be able to help reporters with their work. Customers can call, leave a voice message, and if they like, even talk to a reporter about their situation, he says.

Application Activity
Scoping Out the One-to-One Future

1. Our opening story talks of "discontinuity" or "paradigm shifts" that literally change the world. List three other discontinuities you are aware of other than electronic technology. For each, describe three or more major changes that have resulted.

2. Among the most important determinants of customer satisfaction is the availability of feedback. Describe five ways organizations and individuals can increase their capabilities for gathering useful feedback.

3. Describe at least three examples of how businesses you know are using one-to-one communication to build a stronger relationship with you. (Note: Often these are little things done to build rapport and loyalty.)

-------------------- *Summary of Key Ideas* --------------------

◆ Today's business world is experiencing some important paradigm shifts, especially in the direction of increased personalization of products and services.

◆ Because of advances in technology, one-to-one marketing and customer service will become the standard for businesses in the coming years.

◆ Other changes will continue to arise from social and economic shifts, media choice expansion, and increased interactivity.

◆ Ultimately, much customer service success will stem from the ability to use relationship marketing to gain a greater "share of the customer" rather than just "share of the market."

◆ Database marketing and contact management systems permit people to reach the most appropriate customers and build relationships with them.

◆ Electronic technologies like internet shopping and virtual reality shopping will call for new creativity in creating and managing customer satisfaction and loyalty.

◆ Ultimately, career success will depend largely on one's sense of stewardship—attitudes and ownership of the ongoing efforts to apply the process of customer service.

NOTES

[1] The author acknowledges with appreciation the work of Clayton Eric Farr in developing an early draft of the part of this chapter dealing with the one-to-one future. Eric is a graduate of Brigham Young University and currently works in sales in Southern California.

[2] Some of this material was adapted from Timm, P. and Stead, J., *Communication Skills for Business and Professions* (Upper Saddle River, NJ: Prentice Hall, 1996), Chapter 1.

[3] Excerpted from Pepper, D. And Rogers, M., *The One to One Future* (New York: Currency-Doubleday, 1993), pp. 3–6. Reprinted with permission.

[4] Pepper and Rogers, p. 14.

[5] Quoted in Zachary, G. P. , "Advertisers Anticipate Interactive Media as Ingenious Means to Court Customers," *Wall Street Journal*, August 17, 1994, P. B1.

[6] Gerber, M. E., *The E Myth Revisited* (New York: HarperCollins, 1995), pp. 188–92.

[7] Pepper, D. and Rogers, M., *The One to One Future* (New York: Doubleday, 1993), pp. 18–51.

[8] Sewell, C. and Brown, P. B. *Customers for Life* (New York: Pocket Books, 1990) p. 162.

[9] Pepper and Rogers, p. 37-38.

[10] Griffin, J., *Customer Loyalty: How to Earn It; How to Keep It* (New York: Lexington Books, 1995) p. 125.

[11] Pepper and Rogers, pp. 39–40.

[12]Block, Peter, "Choosing Service over Self-Interest," *Executive Excellence,* August 1993, p. 20.

[13]Excerpted from Johnson, R. "Advancing Technologies Change Perceptions About One-Size-Fits-All Products and Services," *The Service Edge*, Vol. 7, No. 7, July 1994, pp. 1–3. Reprinted with permission of Lakewood Publications.

Index